# CRADLE
# OF
# CIVILIZATION

TIME
LIFE
BOOKS
®

LIFE WORLD LIBRARY

LIFE NATURE LIBRARY

TIME READING PROGRAM

THE LIFE HISTORY OF THE UNITED STATES

LIFE SCIENCE LIBRARY

INTERNATIONAL BOOK SOCIETY

GREAT AGES OF MAN

TIME-LIFE LIBRARY OF ART

TIME-LIFE LIBRARY OF AMERICA

GREAT AGES OF MAN

*A History of the World's Cultures*

# CRADLE
# OF
# CIVILIZATION

by

SAMUEL NOAH KRAMER

and

The Editors of TIME-LIFE BOOKS

TIME INCORPORATED, NEW YORK

THE AUTHOR: Samuel Noah Kramer is one of the world's foremost scholars of Mesopotamian cultures and the cuneiform writing that they used. He received his doctorate from the University of Pennsylvania in 1929 and took part in archeological expeditions to the Middle East in 1930-1931; since 1949 he has served as the University's Clark Research Professor of Assyriology and as curator of the museum's Tablet Collection. Professor Kramer is the author of a number of books, including *History Begins at Sumer*, *The Sumerians: Their Character, History and Culture* and *Biblical Parallels from Sumerian Literature*.

THE CONSULTING EDITOR: Leonard Krieger, University Professor at the University of Chicago, was formerly Professor of History at Yale. Dr. Krieger is the author of *The German Idea of Freedom* and *The Politics of Discretion* and co-author of *History*, written in collaboration with John Higham and Felix Gilbert.

THE COVER: Gypsum figurines, their huge eyes symbolizing awed adoration of Sumerian gods, served busy worshipers as stand-ins at the altar 5,000 years ago.

TIME-LIFE BOOKS

EDITOR
Maitland A. Edey
EXECUTIVE EDITOR
Jerry Korn
TEXT DIRECTOR        ART DIRECTOR
Martin Mann        Sheldon Cotler
CHIEF OF RESEARCH
Beatrice T. Dobie
PICTURE EDITOR
Robert G. Mason
*Assistant Text Directors:*
Harold C. Field, Ogden Tanner
*Assistant Art Director:* Arnold C. Holeywell
*Assistant Chief of Research:* Martha Turner

PUBLISHER
Rhett Austell
*General Manager:* Joseph C. Hazen Jr.
*Circulation Director:* Joan D. Manley
*Marketing Director:* Carter Smith
*Business Manager:* John D. McSweeney
*Publishing Board:* Nicholas Benton,
Louis Bronzo, James Wendell Forbes

GREAT AGES OF MAN
*Series Editor:* Russell Bourne
Editorial Staff for *Cradle of Civilization:*
*Deputy Editor:* Carlotta Kerwin
*Assistant Editor:* Betsy Frankel
*Text Editor:* Robert Tschirky
*Picture Editor:* John Paul Porter
*Designer:* William Rose
*Assistant Designer:* Raymond Ripper
*Staff Writers:* Sam Halper, Bryce Walker,
Edmund White
*Chief Researcher:* Peggy Bushong
*Researchers:* Kathleen Brandes,
Johanna Zacharias, Ann Hersey,
Helen Lapham, Alice Baker, Paula
Norworth, Alice Kantor, Rhea Padis,
Peter Dewitz, Arlene Zuckerman
*Art Assistant:* Anne Landry

EDITORIAL PRODUCTION
*Color Director:* Robert L. Young
*Assistant:* James J. Cox
*Copy Staff:* Marian Gordon Goldman,
Barbara Hults, Florence Keith
*Picture Department:* Dolores A. Littles,
Barbara Sullivan
*Traffic:* Douglas B. Graham

The following individuals and departments of Time Inc. gave valuable aid in the preparation of this book: the Chief of the LIFE Picture Library, Doris O'Neil; the Chief of the Time Inc. Bureau of Editorial Reference, Peter Draz; the Chief of the TIME-LIFE News Service, Richard M. Clurman; Correspondents Barbara Moir and Margot Hapgood (London), Maria Vincenza Aloisi (Paris), Elisabeth Kraemer and Lexi Blomeyer (Bonn), Ann Natanson (Rome), Lee Griggs (Beirut) and Parviz Raein (Tehran).

# CONTENTS

# INTRODUCTION

The story told in the following pages is of buried treasure in cities of long ago.

The treasure is real, as a glance at the illustrations will show: gold, silver, exquisitely carved ivories, gems cut in carnelian, serpentine, lapis lazuli. And yet that seems the least of it. The exciting, the immeasurable value of this treasure goes beyond costly materials. It lies in the unique knowledge these finds bring us: every fragment unearthed from the ancient sites recovers a part of human history that was lost, tells of beginnings, of the first cities ever built, of the first civilized men who lived in them, of their thoughts and doings when the world was new and theirs to subdue.

The cities of long ago from which the treasure comes are the cities of Sumer, of Babylonia and of Assyria. They lie now as low grey mounds in the desert in Iraq, the ancient land of Mesopotamia; what Jeremiah prophesied about them (Jer. 51:43) has indeed come true: "Her cities are a desolation, a dry land, and a wilderness, a land wherein no man dwelleth, neither doth any son of man pass thereby." That anyone should imagine that things remained in them is a wonder.

But someone did. Imaginative explorers began to probe mound after mound around the middle of the last century, and soon brought to light buried palaces and temples. In the south, in ancient Sumer, excavators came upon the statues of Gudea and other striking works of Sumerian art. In the north, in the cities of Assyria, they found colossal human-headed bulls of alabaster and a wealth of narrative reliefs depicting the campaigns of Assyrian kings. The famous library of Assurbanipal, written on clay tablets, turned up in Nineveh; with delight and amazement the world read long-lost Assyrian accounts of wars mentioned in the Bible, and the magnificent *Epic of Gilgamesh* with its heroic quest for eternal life and its story of the Flood so very like the Biblical one.

The early excavations, undertaken to find striking objects to grace museums, were often unmethodical and unobservant. Not until the turn of the century was order and method introduced and due attention paid to architectural remains. A little later on, after the First World War, the supreme importance of careful stratigraphical observation became clear to the excavators. Those years saw, besides the spectacular finds of the royal graves at Ur, a new attention to previously overlooked details that soon extended our knowledge of ancient Mesopotamia back through the millennia of hitherto unknown periods and undreamed-of cultures.

The new emphasis on systematic investigation, and the results achieved through it, shifted the focus of interest. Where earlier scholars had delighted primarily in the new light shed on the Bible, now an additional importance of the excavations became apparent: the light they shed on the beginnings of history. No civilization existed anywhere on the earth's surface before 3000 B.C. Only then did one develop, first in Mesopotamia, a little later in Egypt.

It is this new focus—the view of Mesopotamia as the Cradle of Civilization, as man's first experience of the larger life—that governs the presentation in this volume. Here the achievements of early man follow closely on one another: the invention of writing; the perfection of art as seen in the victory stele of Naram-Sin; the development of law to the level attested to in the Code of Hammurabi; achievements of early mathematicians, astronomers, linguists and, perhaps most of all, of the poets and writers who created the world's first literature—the rich, varied and profound literature of the Sumerians.

For all of this no more delightful and devoted guide could be had than Dr. Kramer. Dean of the world's Sumerologists, and the scholar who has done more than anyone else to recover and make available Sumerian literature, Dr. Kramer is also a most outspoken admirer and loyal defender of the ancient civilization that he here so vividly re-creates.

THORKILD JACOBSEN
*Professor of Assyriology, Harvard University*

ANATOLIA

TAURUS MTS.

AMANUS MTS.

CARCHEMISH

SYRIA

TELL HALAF

TELL BRAK

ARME

CYPRUS

UGARIT

Khabur R.

MEDITERRANEAN SEA

BYBLOS

SYRIAN DESERT

MARI

PALESTINE

JERICHO

DEAD
SEA

RED SEA

*A tablet
showing sites and cities
of the*
CRADLE OF CIVILIZATION

MODERN CITY

ARCHEOLOGICAL SITE

ANCIENT CITY

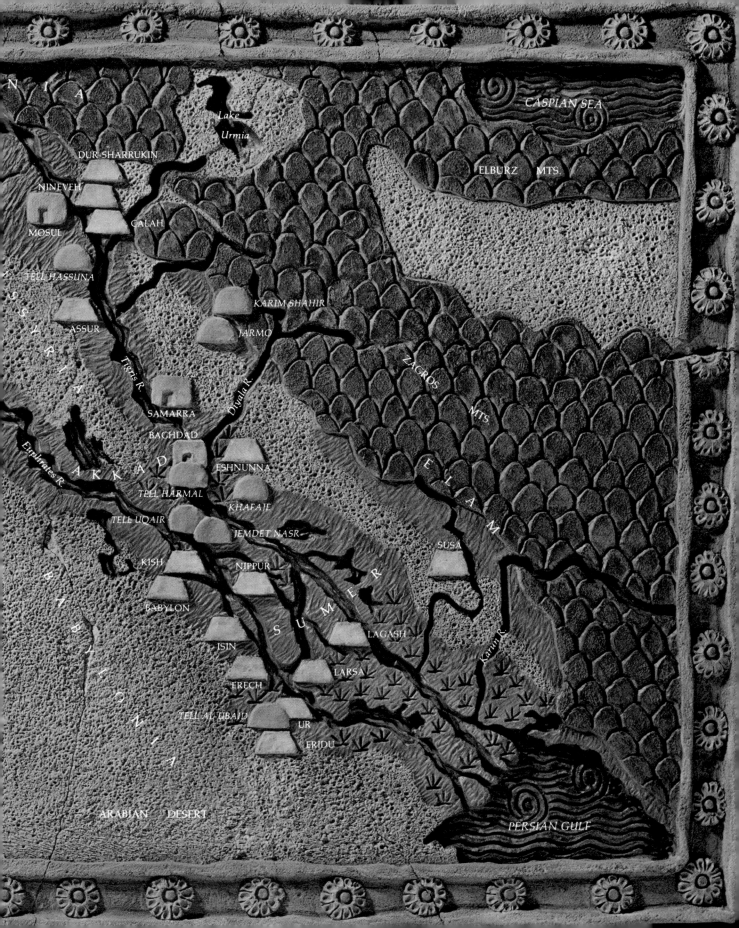

# 1

# THE LAND
# BETWEEN THE RIVERS

Except for reedy swamps and marshes where the Tigris and Euphrates empty into the Persian Gulf, Mesopotamia—the "Land Between the Rivers" of the ancient Greek historians and roughly identical with modern Iraq—consists for its greater part of a bleak alluvial plain. Its climate, by and large, is hot and dry. There are no minerals and almost no stone or timber for building; its soil, if unattended, is arid and sterile.

But unprepossessing though this region appears today, no other place on earth holds deeper significance for the history of human progress. In this land cradled by the rivers man first became civilized. Here, some 5,000 years ago, a people known as the Sumerians developed the world's earliest true civilization from roots extending far back into the dimness of prehistory. It was Mesopotamia that saw the rise of man's first urban centers with their rich, complex and varied life, where political loyalty was no longer to the tribe or clan but to the community as a whole; where lofty ziggurats, or temple-towers, rose skyward, filling the citizen's heart with awe, wonder and pride; where art and technological ingenuity, industrial specialization and commercial enterprise found room to grow and expand.

Perhaps more important, it was in Mesopotamia's early cities that a practical system of writing was first invented and developed, bringing about a revolution in communications that had far-reaching effects on man's economic, intellectual and cultural progress. Ideas, techniques and inventions originated by the Sumerians and nurtured by later Mesopotamian peoples—the Babylonians, Assyrians and others—were diffused east and west to leave their mark on practically all the cultures of antiquity and even on those of our own day.

Mesopotamia's key role in the saga of civilization has become known only in recent times, although it was long recognized that great empires had once flourished there. The Old Testament is full of references to them, and as early as the 12th Century Europeans traveling in the Near East were bringing back reports of ruined cities hidden beneath the rounded mounds of rubble strewn across the Tigris-Euphrates plain. In the 19th Century, when a rage for antiquities swept Europe, excavators began to probe the mysterious mounds, and as a result of their digging, the splendors of fabled Babylon, Dur-Sharrukin, Nineveh and other ancient centers were revealed.

But these pioneer and generally untrained excavators, mostly French and British, were searching chiefly for impressive relics; they paid little attention to the seemingly insignificant details that also help to fill in the picture of the past. Discovery of Mesopotamia's unique significance in human history, therefore, had to wait until digging in the Near East ceased to be a treasure hunt and became a discipline. The turning point came around the beginning of the present century when professional archeologists started to replace the relic seekers, and enthusiastic but slipshod excavating methods gave way to highly refined techniques. By about 1920 Near Eastern archeology was on a fully scientific footing—and only then did excavators begin the systematic unearthing of Mesopotamian villages as well as cities, huts as well as palaces, pots and tools as well as monumental sculptures.

In reconstructing Mesopotamia's history and culture and the life and character of its people, scholars have been aided immeasurably by the thousands upon thousands of inscribed clay tablets turned up in the excavations and deciphered. These records, written in wedge-shaped cuneiform characters, shed light on nearly every aspect of ancient existence, from the sonorous proclamations of kings to the inventory of a merchant's warehouse, from literary and religious works to a father's admonitions to his wayward son.

The two decades following 1920 and archeology's coming of age in Mesopotamia were marked by one momentous find after another. At Ur—the Bible's "Ur of the Chaldees"—in southern Mesopotamia, the British archeologist Sir Leonard Woolley was opening so-called royal tombs of the Third Millennium B.C. with spectacular results. The world

was amazed at their wealth of breathtaking objects of gold, silver and lapis lazuli and shocked by their remains of retainers who had apparently been buried alive. Some 50 miles to the northwest, Sumerian temples on lofty platforms and dating from as early as 3000 B.C. were emerging from the ground inch by inch as German archeologists probed the site of Biblical Erech. Found among the ruins were hundreds of clay tablets inscribed with pictographic signs, the forerunners of cuneiform writing. Still farther north, in the mound that had been Kish, a major city of ancient Sumer, an Anglo-American team was uncovering monumental buildings, ziggurats and cemeteries, and from a smaller nearby mound came tablets that provided additional links in the development of writing.

In central Mesopotamia, northeast of Baghdad, an American expedition was finding temples, palaces and private houses of cities about which almost nothing had been known, and with them sculptures in the round created about 2700 B.C., among the earliest works of their kind discovered in Mesopotamia. More than 200 miles westward, in Syria and just across the Iraqi border, French excavators were beginning to unearth Mari, a city laid waste by conquerors 37 centuries ago. One of its most imposing ruins was a royal palace that covered nearly seven acres.

While these astonishing discoveries were being made, other excavators, stripping layer after layer of earth from sites of even greater antiquity, were slowly pushing back the horizon of Mesopotamian prehistory. And far from Mesopotamia and its buried cities, in the Oriental Institute of the University of Chicago, a vast cooperative enterprise had been set in motion to analyze and translate every word and phrase inscribed on the thousands of cuneiform tablets in museums the world over.

The rich discoveries and fruitful studies of these productive decades, and of the decades since, have made it more and more evident that Mesopotamia, rather than any other land or region, merits being called the "Cradle of Civilization."

Civilization came rather late in man's career —around 3000 B.C. Behind its birth lay a long prelude—the countless formative centuries during which the homeless, solitary hunter of wild beasts and gatherer of wild plants learned to live in hamlet and village, to domesticate animals and cultivate crops. With fields and herds to provide fairly reliable sustenance, and neighbors to share his work, man for the first time could enjoy leisure in which to develop rudimentary arts, techniques and ideas and to invent new ones. It was these advances that made man civilized. This revolutionary change from nomadic parasite to sedentary producer took place about 10,000 years ago. As to the place where it occurred, experts once speculated that it must be Mesopotamia. Since Mesopotamia was conceded to be the seat of man's "urban revolution," it seemed reasonable to surmise that it may have been the seat of his "economic revolution" as well, and that somewhere in this region agriculture and animal domestication originated.

The pioneer in attempting to trace to its source this momentous but obscure turning point in human events was Robert J. Braidwood of the University of Chicago. Man, Braidwood reasoned, may indeed have built his first cities in Mesopotamia's nearly rainless south after he had learned to drain and irrigate its reed-filled swamps and marshes. But the first agricultural hamlets and villages must have arisen in the north, on the hilly flanks of the Zagros ranges, in the region now commonly known as Kurdistan, where there was ample rainfall, where wheat and barley grew wild, and where wild ancestors of sheep, goats, cattle and pigs were plentiful. It was in this area, hardly touched by archeologists, that Braidwood expected to discover traces of the world's earliest farmers and cattle breeders.

Braidwood's opportunity to demonstrate the validity of his "hilly flanks" theory came in 1948, but it did not come easily. Up to that time most excavations in Mesopotamia, sponsored by university and museum trustees who expected impressive returns for the money spent, were still centered largely on the glamorous city-mounds or "tells" (Arabic for ruin-mounds) to the south. These guaranteed a yield of such precious objects as written tablets and art treasures, while the smaller northern mounds promised only meager returns in the form of crude, uninscribed artifacts.

Braidwood, therefore, had to create his opportunity. Persistent, persevering and persuasive, he finally convinced authorities of the University of Chicago that the principal aim of digging in the Near East was not to bring back museum pieces for display, but to help clarify the step-by-step process of man's cultural progress over the millennia; that one of the most significant and fundamental of these steps was the transition from food-collecting to food-producing; and that the key to the time and place of this development would more likely be found in the uninviting mounds of Kurdistan than in the spectacular city-mounds farther south.

For his first major excavation Braidwood picked a three-acre site called Jarmo, situated in the foothills of the northern Zagros, and dug there for several seasons. From the beginning he struck archeological pay dirt. Digging down through the mound to virgin soil, he identified 15 superimposed levels of human occupation. The lowest 10 were preceramic—that is, their inhabitants seemed to have been so primitive that they knew nothing of baked clay vessels and their advantages for domestic use. Even so, they were sufficiently advanced to build rectangular mud houses of several rooms each and to provide them with ovens, chimneys and clay-lined hearths sunk below ground level. That they were skilled stoneworkers was evident from objects found lying about the rooms, among them stone axes with polished cutting edges, stone spindle whorls (indicating some knowledge of weaving) and elegantly ground limestone cups and bowls. From the bones of animals they fashioned awls and needles. They adorned their bodies with necklaces, bracelets, rings and pendants of stone, bone or clay, and they modeled unfired clay figurines.

What was important for the history of agriculture, however, was the mound's yield in carbonized form of two kinds of cultivated wheat, emmer and einkorn, as well as a cultivated barley and several varieties of peas and beans. Also, the implements of stone included such farming tools as pestles and mortars for pounding grain, and flint sickle blades. Nearly all animal bones were those of the domesticated, or domesticable, goat, sheep, cattle and dog.

In short, at Jarmo Braidwood had uncovered the oldest permanent farming community then known —a village dating to about 7000 B.C. and so backward that only its very latest inhabitants were acquainted with pottery making, a craft practiced in the most primitive villages previously excavated in the Near East. But backward as it was, its predominant economy had been a relatively advanced stage of agriculture.

Though Jarmo had thus proved immensely significant for the light it shed on the very early days of farming, it had not resolved the fundamental problem of the time and place of agriculture's origin. Since farming had been in full swing throughout the village's occupation—which may have lasted 400 years—Braidwood needed a settlement older than Jarmo to discover traces of agriculture's incipient and more rudimentary stages. A nearby site, Karim Shahir, showed surface signs of being more primitive, and Braidwood dug there next.

Unlike many-layered Jarmo, Karim Shahir turned out to have only a single level of occupation. In its remains, Braidwood found such clues to agricul-

tural activity as stone hoes, grinding stones and flint sickle blades as well as many bones of domesticable animals. But there were no vestiges of any cereals or of any identifiable house plans; the site seemed to have been a camping ground of a seminomadic people who may have practiced a crude kind of hoe-farming and moved on as the soil became exhausted. Karim Shahir gave the appearance of a place many centuries older than Jarmo, and one where agriculture was indeed in its infancy.

Braidwood's carefully planned excavations had now revealed two sites of crucial importance for the earliest history of agriculture. The short-lived encampment of Karim Shahir, with its evidence of incipient farming, lent weight to the surmise that Mesopotamia had witnessed agriculture's birth and at the same time it strengthened Braidwood's contention that the flanks of the northern Zagros had been its birthplace. And since Jarmo was the most ancient farming village yet discovered, it seemed likely that it was Mesopotamia too that saw man's transition to a food-producing economy and the settled life that it entailed.

This was the generally accepted picture in 1951. Then archeologists turned to some of the lands neighboring on Mesopotamia—and made discoveries that threaten not only to topple Braidwood's "hilly flanks" hypothesis for the origin of agriculture, but also to undermine Mesopotamia's standing as the probable home of the economic revolution (though not, of course, as the birthplace of the city). Evidence from excavations in Palestine, Syria, Turkish Anatolia and Iran indicates that agriculture's inception, as well as the first communal life based on farming, may actually have occurred in these areas, and earlier than in Mesopotamia.

One impressive piece of evidence comes from Jericho, the famous Biblical city that had its site on a mound near the northern end of the Dead Sea in Palestine, a region separated from Mesopotamia by the vast Syrian Desert. Not only is Jericho not perched on a "hilly flank," but it also lies sunk in a valley almost a thousand feet below sea level, one of the driest spots on earth. But flowing nearby is a spring whose waters turn the surrounding terrain into a green oasis.

Between 1952 and 1958 archeologists, peeling off layer after layer of Jericho's mound, laid bare a remarkable preceramic town covering 10 acres and enclosed by a wall of massive undressed stones. Although no grain or domesticated animals could be identified among the ruins, the presence of grinding stones, mortars and pestles pointed to an incipient agriculture, effective enough to feed an estimated population of 2,000 or more.

More astonishing than the town's great size was its apparent antiquity. According to carbon 14 tests (which measure the extent of decay of radioactive carbon in such organic remains as charcoal and bone), most of the town dated back probably to the beginning of the Eighth Millennium B.C. or earlier. Thus Jericho, in its low-lying valley, had evidently accomplished the changeover from food-collecting to food-producing and settled life long before 7000 B.C., when Jarmo emerged as a village in the hills of northern Mesopotamia.

But whether or not Mesopotamia must ultimately surrender its claim to be the birthplace of agriculture and the site of man's economic revolution, there is no question that it was the land where farming first developed into a solid base for civilization and the rise of cities. For once agriculture spread from the highlands around Jarmo into the upper reaches of the Tigris-Euphrates plain, it found in the alluvium laid down by the rivers a soil uniquely favorable to its future growth.

How did this changeover from parasitic hunter to productive farmer occur—and why? Psychologically, it seems curious and anomalous for a foot-loose hunter to surrender his heritage of free-roving mobility and let himself be bound to earth and hearth, all for a mess of peasant's pottage.

In all probability, however, it was not the confident, self-sufficient and well-adapted among the nomads who let themselves be beguiled by the dubious promise of sedentary life. Rather it was the dissatisfied, the weak and the despised who broke away from their more successful and oppressive fellows and made the first awkward and halting attempts to settle down and wrest a living from the soil. Women, too, no doubt played a role in making man a stay-at-home. To many of them the advantages of rearing children in a fixed home must have been apparent, and some of the more articulate and persistent may well have been instrumental in persuading their spouses to settle down, at least for a time. Another factor may have been a scarcity of game and edible wild plants, in regions where they had once been abundant.

In any case, once started, agriculture began to turn the weak into the strong, the listless into enterprising producers, the few into the many. And with the gradual development and improvement of farming techniques over the millennia there came an immense proliferation of hamlet, village and town all over the ancient world, and especially in northern Mesopotamia.

Between the farmers of 9,000-year-old Jarmo and the next known people who played a significant role in Mesopotamia's trend toward civilization stretches a gap of several obscure centuries. From about the middle of the Sixth Millennium onward, however, the successive stages in this long progression sparked by agriculture become less shadowy, as fairly well-defined cultures begin to emerge. Since writing still lay far in the future, each speaks for itself through its distinctive pottery and other material remains.

The earliest of these cultures, dating roughly

from 5800 B.C., is named Hassuna after the mound near modern Mosul where it was first recognized in the 1940s by archeologists of Iraq's Directorate-General of Antiquities. The original inhabitants of Hassuna itself seem to have been seminomads who combined a primitive sort of farming with food-collecting, stored their grain in crude pottery vessels reminiscent of those used by Jarmo's latest occupants, and lived in temporary shelters that left no traces. But after several generations the Hassuna people, apparently induced by more efficient agricultural methods, abandoned their nomadic ways to dwell in villages of well-built, rectangular adobe houses consisting of as many as six or seven rooms arranged around a courtyard and remarkably similar to the homes of present-day Iraqi peasants. Grain was kept in huge clay bins sunk into the earth, and some of the ancient houses had domed ovens for baking bread.

With improved dwellings came refinements in pottery; although still crude, it began to show burnished surfaces or simple painted designs. In late Hassuna times a far superior polychrome pottery made its appearance alongside these rather coarse products. For beauty and intricacy of decoration —which included plants, animals and human figures —this pottery was never again equaled in ancient Mesopotamia. Generally known as "Samarra" ware, because it was first discovered underlying the ruins of Samarra, the city north of Baghdad that was the capital of the Abbasid caliphate in the Ninth Century A.D., the pottery may reflect either a migration of highly skilled people from beyond the Zagros Mountains or a local technological and esthetic achievement.

Possibly spurred by a surplus of grain for barter, trade with distant parts of the prehistoric world began to expand, and evidence of this is found in artifacts scattered in the remains of Hassuna settlements. Obsidian for tools and other implements,

for example, came from the vicinity of Lake Van in eastern Turkey, its nearest source. Antimony and malachite for making eye paint and semiprecious stones for beads and pendants were imported from Iran, and shells for ornaments were obtained from the Persian Gulf region.

Around 5000 B.C. the Hassuna people faded out of the picture and a new culture arose to dominate the stage in northern Mesopotamia for the next thousand years. First traces of it were unearthed at Tell Halaf in northeastern Syria, and its advent marked a quickening in the pace of progress. Vigorous and inventive, this Halafian culture ushered in advances in various fields and spread its influence in a great arc reaching from the foothills of the northern Zagros to the Mediterranean.

Fostered by industrious Halaf farmers, agriculture prospered. A wider variety of grain was cultivated than ever before and herds of cattle and goats could be seen grazing in the fields outside the villages, some of which now boasted such public works as cobbled streets. There were signs, too, that another change was in the making, one that would eventually prove almost as dynamic and far-reaching as the transition to settled farming life. Occasional implements and beads of copper found among the stone tools at Halafian sites heralded the approaching end of the Stone Age in the Near East and the dawn of the Age of Metals.

But as ironic fate would have it, the progress and unprecedented prosperity that the economic revolution had brought to the proliferating northern villages also brought in its wake new groups of the depressed and oppressed, the disgruntled and dissatisfied. These malcontents had nothing to lose and everything to gain by breaking away from their neighbors and emigrating to the marshlands of southern Mesopotamia, little dreaming that in the course of time their offspring would transform it into a Cradle of Civilization.

A SILHOUETTED MOUND, *rising above the remains of the Sumerian city of Nippur, is a principal site of archeological excavation in Mesopotamia.*

# UNEARTHING THE PAST

Before archeologists began to dig in Mesopotamia, almost nothing was known of the empires that flourished there 4,500 years ago. The Bible and works of Greek and Roman historians had made brief mention of the Babylonians and the Assyrians, but the information was vague and contradictory. Of a still older people, the Sumerians, nothing at all was known—not even the fact that they had existed.

The main reason the peoples of Mesopotamia remained forgotten for so long was that they, unlike the Egyptians and other ancient empire-builders, had not built in enduring stone but in mud brick. Rain, annual floods and shifting sands slowly leveled the bricks and buried the towers and palaces, leaving only shapeless mounds. For thousands of years no one was aware of the secrets these mounds concealed, but in the middle of the 19th Century, French, German and English archeologists started to explore them. Within a few years the spade revealed some remarkable facts: Mesopotamians were the first people on earth to live in cities, study the stars, use the arch and wheeled vehicles, write epic poetry and compile a legal code. Today the pursuit of the past continues at sites like Nippur *(above)*, the religious capital of Sumer. By scientifically analyzing ruined buildings, broken pottery and clay tablets, archeologists are compiling an increasingly complete picture of the world's first known civilization.

*Photographs by Georg Gerster*

A BASTION OF CIVILIZATION, *the mound of the city of Nippur rises out of the windswept desert. The structure on top, built by American archeologist*

bout 1900, crowns the ruined ziggurat, or temple-tower. In ancient times Nippur was on the Euphrates, surrounded not by desert but by irrigated fields.

# AN ARMY OF
# EXPERT DIGGERS

A modern archeological team is divided into task forces, each with its appointed duties. Leading the expedition at Nippur are four professional archeologists who are in charge of some 110 men, a team slightly smaller than the average one in Mesopotamia. One professional must have a knowledge of architecture so as to be able to interpret ruins. The architect at Nippur is also the field director, James E. Knudstad of the University of Chicago, shown standing alone in the foreground. Behind him, from right to left, are a surveyor, who draws plans of the site; a photographer, who takes pictures of all major finds; an epigrapher, who translates cuneiform tablets; and a representative of the Iraqi Department of Antiquities, who reports on the team's progress.

Behind the Iraqi representative is the foreman of the laborers; behind him are the skilled diggers and the men who convey sand away in carts. The service staff— cook, driver, waiters, watchmen—surrounds the Landrover vehicle at right. Behind the Landrover stand the heavy pick-handlers and, to the left of them, the shovelmen. In the background are the workers who haul sand out of excavated areas in burlap bags.

DEEPENING A TRENCH, *laborers haul sand out of an excavation at Nippur and deposit it in carts, which are pushed on tracks to a distant dump.*

# UNCOVERING AND CHARTING THE STRATA OF HISTORY

A basic aim of archeology is to establish the chronology of a site. To do this, excavators determine where each layer of structures, representing a historical period, begins and ends, then mark off these levels. The problem is especially difficult in Mesopotamia since the basic building material, mud brick, is sometimes scarcely distinguishable from the earth it is buried in. To bring out the differences, archeologists resort to many techniques, from wetting the ground and looking for variations in color to studying samples of debris and noting differences in grain and porosity.

After a level is defined, excavators try to determine its age by studying the evidence in it. A dated inscription, or a seal or tablet giving a king's name, may indicate which period the level represents. Once one object has been dated, archeologists can usually assume that other objects in the level were made at the same time —and are thus able to get a glimpse of the life of any given era.

LABELING LAYERS, *an archeologist fixes tags on an excavated wall that was rebuilt many times over the ages.*

EXPOSING PAVEMENT, *a workman removes dirt and debris. By uncovering streets and squares archeologists gradually reveal the basic plan of a city.*

GATHERING TO SEE A DISCOVERY, *excavators peer down a shaft. As a digger was clearing the shaft of fill, he came across the tablet shown at right.*

# PRESERVING A FIND

Written tablets are the most informative artifacts that archeologists can discover in Mesopotamia, and when one is found it is treated with great care. Most tablets are of unbaked clay, and if they have been buried in damp soil, they are as soft as cheese; they must be cautiously removed from surrounding rubble and their inscriptions preserved by firing. Each tablet is placed in a container filled with a protective matrix of sand and baked in a kiln. When cool and hard, the tablet is cleaned by sandblasting. Finally, a latex rubber impression is made of the inscription; many plaster casts can then be prepared from this mold and sent to be studied by archeologists all over the world.

FREEING THE TABLET, *a workman loosens the hard-packed dirt with a flat knife and removes it with an ordinary paintbrush.*

A LATEX MOLD *is peeled off the baked and cleaned tablet, which bears a part of a 3,000-year-old copy of an even older literary text.*

# POTTERY: "ABC" OF ARCHEOLOGY

Water jugs, storage vases, drinking vessels and dishes are among the most numerous finds on any archeological site; few, however, are found intact. In the pictures at right an expert cleans the shards of a Sumerian jug with a scraper, applies glue to them, and finally completes the assembly.

If the pot turns out to be a known type, it can be used to date the other objects found around it. If it can be proved to have come from another country, its presence in Mesopotamia indicates contact between the two civilizations. By closely analyzing the texture or glaze of the pottery an expert can tell at what temperature the vessel was fired and whether it was turned on a wheel, which in turn suggests the level of technology achieved by its makers.

In some cases pottery also preserves the designs of other ancient wares that may have rotted away over the centuries; since clay is easily worked, potters freely imitated motifs that had originally been used in weaving, leather or basketwork. Indeed, so much can be deduced from simple bowls or vases that pottery has been called the "alphabet" of archeology.

A FLYING CAMERA, *taking pictures like the one at right, is suspended from a kite over Erech, 65 miles from Nippur.*

# NEW TECHNIQUES

In recent years science has contributed much to archeology. Aerial views, like that of Erech at right, taken by a radio-controlled camera fitted with a "fisheye" lens and rigged on a kite, permit archeologists to see a city's over-all plan. (The picture shows the mound of the ziggurat in the center and the partially excavated city around it.) The camera can also spot variations in soil or plant growth that may indicate a buried wall or tomb. Another technique, derived from nuclear science, dates organic substances by their carbon content *(see Appendix)*, while mine detectors and echo-ranging instruments locate buried artifacts and structures.

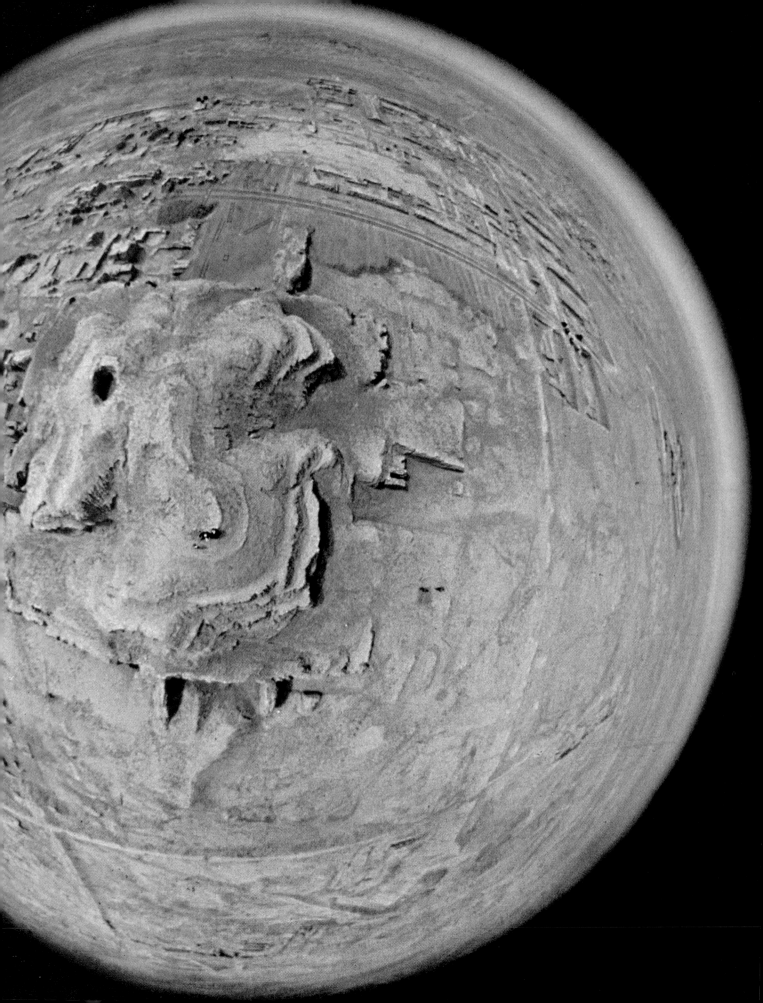

# 2
# MAN'S FIRST CITIES

It was not a land flowing with milk and honey that greeted the farmers who, early in the Fifth Millennium B.C., abandoned their villages in northern Mesopotamia and emigrated southward in search of a new and happier home.

In the part of the Tigris-Euphrates plain that was to become known first as Sumer and later as Babylonia—the region stretching from present-day Baghdad to the Persian Gulf—the pioneer colonists found the soil baked stone-hard during the long, cruelly hot summer. All vegetation withered under the scorching sun, and day after relentless day a searing wind out of the northwest blew up a powdery, choking dust that invaded every exposed pore of the body.

Then came the winter with its stormy south wind that brought cloudy skies and an occasional tempestuous downpour that turned the plain into a slithery morass. In the brief, refreshing spring that followed, the plain was green with low-flowering perennials. Spring was the season, too, when rains and melting snows in the Zagros and other northern ranges swelled the Tigris and Euphrates to flood level, and from time to time the rivers overflowed their channels to submerge the plain as far as the eye could see. More than one unwary immigrant no doubt lost all his possessions and perhaps even his life in such unpredictable and catastrophic inundations.

But bleak and dismal as the region may have seemed to the weary homeseekers, it had one overriding attraction. Strung all along the southern reaches of the meandering Euphrates and dominating the low-lying plain were natural levees built up over the millennia by the river as it repeatedly overtopped its banks. The levees, with their gentle backslopes of coarse-textured silt and sediment, lent themselves readily to draining, planting and cultivation and so were ideal for the simple agriculture practiced by these early farmers. Then, too, not very far from the levees were numerous reed-covered swamps and marshes that teemed with fish and waterfowl during much of the year and that in springtime provided excellent forage for herds of sheep and goats. It is not surprising, therefore, that it was on the promising Euphrates levees and in the nearby marshlands that the wanderers decided to settle down; here they unloaded their clay pots, their stone tools and the priceless seeds they had brought with them from the north.

These earliest inhabitants of southern Mesopotamia are known as Ubaidians, from Tell al-Ubaid, a small mound near the ruined city of Ur, where their remains were first found about 50 years ago. The single thin layer of primitive artifacts unearthed there led archeologists to conclude at first that the Ubaid period of occupation had been quite short and that the Ubaidians were crude marsh dwellers who could build nothing better than mud-plastered reed huts to shelter themselves.

More recently discovered Ubaidian remains, however, have proved this picture to be false. Today the early settlers along the river levees are recognized as able and enterprising farmers who prospered and multiplied over the centuries. They scattered the Tigris-Euphrates plain with villages and towns built of mud bricks, since stone was scarce, and counted large and complex mud-brick temples among their accomplishments. By 4000 B.C. they had become an important civilizing force not only in southern Mesopotamia but to some extent throughout the ancient Near East; traces of their culture have been found from the Mediterranean to regions beyond the Zagros and as far north as the Caspian Sea.

The Ubaidians, moreover, are the first people in the history of man for whose ethnic identity and cultural achievement we have linguistic evidence. To be sure, we do not know what they called themselves since writing was still unknown in their day, but clay documents of later Sumerian times make it apparent that they were not Sumerians. For example, the names by which the document writers referred to the Tigris and Euphrates —*Idiglat* and *Buranun*—are not Sumerian words and are therefore generally assumed to be of Ubaidian origin. It must have been the Ubaidians,

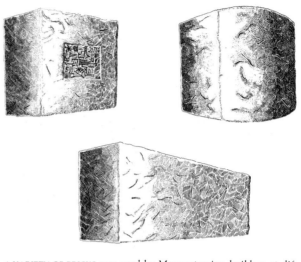

A VARIETY OF BRICKS *was used by Mesopotamian builders at different times. The commonest was a rectangular shape (directly above) made of mud with a straw binder. The Babylonians also molded square units, often bearing inscriptions to their gods (top left), and the Sumerians used loaf-shaped bricks (top right).*

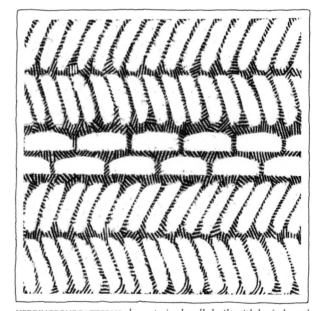

HERRINGBONE PATTERNS *characterized walls built with loaf-shaped Sumerian bricks. Horizontal rows were alternated with bricks set at an angle and cemented with mud or with natural asphalt.*

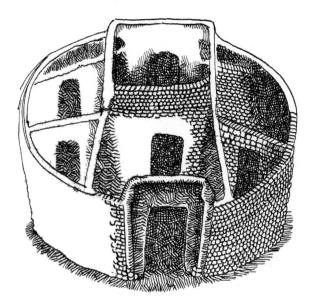

too, who gave such names as Eridu, Ur, Lagash, Nippur and Kish to some of the villages and towns that later developed into large and impressive Sumerian cities. Even more important, it was from the language of this thriving and prosperous people that the Sumerians probably borrowed such culturally significant words as farmer, herdsman, plow, metalworker, weaver and carpenter.

But success and achievement breed envy among peoples as well as individuals, and it was not long before rivals appeared to challenge the Ubaidians' standing as the sole occupants of southern Mesopotamia. Around the end of the Fifth Millennium B.C. some of the hordes of Semitic nomads inhabiting the Syrian Desert and the Arabian peninsula to the west began to infiltrate the Ubaidian settlements, both as conquerors in search of booty and as peaceful immigrants eager to better their lot. The resulting cross-fertilization of the two peoples and cultures, the Ubaidian and the Semitic, brought about a new and even more productive era during which it may be said that the foundations were laid for the world's first true civilization.

The builders of that civilization, the Sumerians, did not arrive upon the scene until about 3500 B.C., probably from Central Asia by way of Iran. With the advent of this third important group of people there took place in southern Mesopotamia an ethnic and cultural fusion that was to influence profoundly the future course of humanity. In the centuries that followed, Sumer—as the land came to be called—attained unprecedented heights of material wealth and political power and saw the rise of the world's first cities. It was in these Sumerian cities of the late Fourth and early Third Millennia B.C. that ancient man accomplished some of his most impressive achievements in art and architecture, in social organization, in religious thought and practice and—with the invention of writing—in education and communication.

The cities that came into being in Sumer over 5,000 years ago were the culmination of a long cultural development that began in the hamlets of the earliest Ubaidian settlers. When the first immigrants into southern Mesopotamia settled on the slopes of the Euphrates levees, the seed they planted was quick to yield a rich and manifold return. There were, of course, dark days when the river overflowed its banks so violently that it flooded and drowned everything within its reach. But usually the inundation was moderate and gentle and could readily be channeled into the small canals and primitive reservoirs that even the very earliest Ubaidians learned to construct.

With food plentiful and reasonably assured, families increased in size. The more children to help in the field, the larger the area that could be cultivated, and a hamlet originally consisting of several flimsy reed-and-mud huts gradually grew into a village of mud-brick houses of several rooms each. What had begun as a family enterprise evolved into a small local community in which attachment to place became the prime incentive of all major activity. This shift of loyalty from family to group was a social adjustment without which the birth of cities would have been impossible.

Another factor that strengthened the unity of the

early village was the temple and its service. The immigrants from the north either brought with them or developed not long after their arrival an abiding faith in one special deity as the protector of their settlement, and with the building of their first houses they also erected a home for their divinity. For example, underlying the ruins of Eridu, one of Sumer's most venerated cities, archeologists unearthed a mud-brick temple built on virgin soil by the original Ubaidian inhabitants. It was a small rectangular shrine, about 15 feet long, and its furnishings consisted of nothing more than a crude altar and an offering table. But as the villages prospered through agriculture and expanded into sizable towns, such humble shrines were enlarged into elaborate structures each set atop a lofty mud-brick platform, a prototype of the future ziggurat, or temple-tower. Each temple served an entire community, rather than an individual family or clan, and thus generated and intensified local patriotism, pride and effort.

Nor was the temple merely an edifice of lifeless brick and mortar; it was a holy place that had to be tended and cared for every day, year in and year out. Hymns and prayers had to be composed, formalized and recited; rites and rituals had to be performed; sacred festivals had to be celebrated. And so a specialized priesthood came into being, starting no doubt with the selection of one or two individuals noted for their learning and spiritual powers and proliferating in number and function over the centuries. In the course of time the temple and its priestly coterie naturally became the intellectual center of each community, and it is therefore not surprising that it was in the temple that writing was later invented and developed.

With the prosperity and expansion of southern Mesopotamia's early communities came an increase in the size and number of their farms and fields, and also in their irrigation canals and reservoirs which were essential to the agricultural economy; without them the land would have quickly reverted to barren desert in this virtually rainless region. But irrigation, especially in its more advanced stages, could be effectively carried out only as a community enterprise, not as an individual undertaking. Canals and reservoirs of considerable size had to be excavated, cleaned at regular intervals and kept constantly in repair. In addition, water-rights had to be equitably distributed; boundary lines had to be carefully marked and authenticated; arguments had to be adjudicated and settled.

All these factors led to the gradual establishment of another feature facilitating city growth—a secular administration that began with a limited appointed personnel but ultimately evolved into a formidable bureaucracy with all the advantages and evils that this entails. Surprisingly, the government of the early Mesopotamian villages and towns was democratic; members of the ruling bodies were appointed not by a single omnipotent individual, as one might expect, but by an assembly made up of the community's free citizens.

As long as the communities remained at the village level and land and irrigation conflicts were confined to individuals and families, the secular administration played a minor role in community life. Objectionable and untrustworthy officials could be easily removed from office by the citizens' assemblies that met as the need arose. But, as the villages grew into towns and the towns into cities, each eager to control as much as possible of the rich irrigated land in and about its borders, strife and contention became ever more frequent and violent, and consequences for the loser were often disastrous. What had started as limited economic rivalries turned into bitter political struggles for power, prestige and territory, and the more aggressive among the early cities resorted to warfare in order to achieve their ambitious goals.

Unable to cope with such military threats, the democratic decision-making assemblies that had survived since the days of the village found it necessary to select one of their most capable and courageous citizens to lead them to victory over the enemy. And so the institution of kingship was born. At first the appointment of a "big man"—for that is the literal meaning of *lugal*, the Sumerian word for king—was temporary and his authority limited; at the passing of the military crisis he relinquished his powers and returned to civil life, honored and esteemed for his services. But as one conflict bred another, the role of king lost its transitory character and became hereditary, dynastic and despotic.

Following the establishment of kingship around 3000 B.C., the story of Sumer is largely a tale of warfare as the rulers of its dozen or so city-states, which were bound only by a common language and culture, vied for mastery of the entire region. In succeeding centuries the Tigris-Euphrates plain became the scene of constant battle, a broad stage across which marched a pageant of ancient armies led by warrior-kings with exotic names. A few of the cities engaged in this struggle are familiar to us through the Bible—the Old Testament mentions Erech and "Ur of the Chaldees," traditional birthplace of the Patriarch Abraham—but most of their names sound as strange to modern ears as do those of the kings who assaulted their walls.

Interrupting the cities' almost incessant contest for supremacy were several interludes during which all Sumer was forced to bow to foreigners, but each time foreign domination was shaken off, the rivalry between cities flared up again. This unremitting and exhausting internal strife was a major factor in the ultimate disintegration of Sumer at the beginning of the 18th Century B.C., when the people known to history as Babylonians won ascendancy in Mesopotamia.

The first city to succeed in establishing control over the whole of Sumer was undoubtedly Kish, whose ruins lie 55 miles south of modern Baghdad. Kish seems to have reached its pre-eminence under a king named Etana, who probably reigned toward the beginning of the Third Millennium B.C. This assumption is based upon the Sumerian King List, an amazing document written almost a thousand years after Etana's day and naming most of the rulers of Sumer from the advent of kingship onward. The list describes Etana as he who "stabilized all the lands," and this may mean that under him Kish not only dominated the other Sumerian cities but extended its rule to include some of the neighboring lands as well.

Not long after Etana's reign, Kish began to find a rival for supremacy in the city of Erech, about a hundred miles to the southeast. The founder of Erech's first royal dynasty, Meskiaggasher, appears to have been an even mightier monarch than Etana, for the King List tells that he "entered the sea, ascended the mountains," signifying perhaps that at one time he may have held sway over a region spreading from the Mediterranean to the Zagros Mountains east of Sumer.

Other kings who succeeded Meskiaggasher to the throne of early Erech were also memorable rulers. Several of them left such deep impressions on their subjects that they were deified after death. One, named Dumuzi, became an important fertility god in the Mesopotamian pantheon and his cult eventually influenced other ancient Near Eastern religions as well. The Jews, for example, knew him as Tammuz; as late as the Sixth Century B.C. the women of Jerusalem were still bewailing his death and legendary descent to the underworld, an event that had come to be identified with the annual decline of vegetation. One of the months of the Hebrew calendar to this very day bears Dumuzi's Semitic name of Tammuz.

By far the most famous of Erech's early kings,

however, was Gilgamesh, who is believed to have reigned sometime during the 27th Century B.C. Scores of myths and legends later grew up around the name and exploits of this illustrious king, and in the course of time he became not only a demigod of Mesopotamia and its supreme folk hero, but also one of the towering epic figures of the entire ancient world. Throughout the centuries tales of his conflicts with ferocious beasts and superhuman adversaries and of his quest for the secret of immortality were written and rewritten in Sumerian, Akkadian, Hittite and other languages of the early Near East, and he may well have been the prototype for the Greek hero Heracles.

Celebrated in story and legend though Gilgamesh was, no contemporary records have been found to shed light on the actual events of his life and reign. Later documents, however, indicate that his was an era of political turmoil during which the rulers of the cities of Kish, Ur and Erech carried on a bitter, three-cornered struggle for the hegemony of Sumer. The victor in these internecine hostilities was Gilgamesh of Erech. But it was an empty triumph, for the bloody civil wars had so weakened Sumer that it became a vassal to kings of the Elamites, traditional enemies inhabiting what is now southwestern Iran.

Although several efforts were made by one or another of the Sumerian cities to regain control of the land from the Elamites, it was not until about a century after Gilgamesh that Sumer recovered from its plight. That it did recover is testimony to the remarkable resilience of the Sumerians; without this quality it would not have been possible for them to maintain their civilization through more than a thousand years of alternating conquest and civil discord.

The savior of Sumer was Lugalannemundu, a king of the city of Adab, whose deeds are recorded in an ancient document that describes him as he

"who made all the foreign lands pay steady tribute to him." Lugalannemundu overthrew Elamite rule, and reunited the city-states, but he was not content to stop there. By defeating a confederation of 13 kings controlling between them virtually all of the ancient Near East he made his influence felt far beyond the limits of Sumer. Even the military victories and patriotic efforts of this dynamic man did not, however, bring lasting unity and peace to Sumer. After his death the land was once again split asunder by the chronic rivalry between the city-states, and for the next 200 years Sumer was witness to another cycle in the ceaseless struggle for supremacy.

During that troubled period Lagash, a city-state situated about 35 miles northeast of Erech, became the dominant military and political power in divided Sumer. The story of cities that rose and fell in earlier times is known only from documents written many centuries after the events took place. That of Lagash, on the other hand, is a matter of recorded history that has come down to us through contemporary documents by Lagashite archivists, man's first historiographers.

The ruler whose military conquests raised Lagash to the pinnacle of power around 2450 B.C. was Eannatum, third in that city's first dynasty of kings. Early in his career of aggression Eannatum successfully attacked the neighboring city of Umma, with whom Lagash had repeatedly battled over irrigation rights. To commemorate Umma's defeat he set up as a boundary stone between the two cities a monument called "The Stele of the Vultures," of which a few large fragments still exist, and upon it he ordered inscribed the peace terms that had brought the war to an end—history's earliest known diplomatic treaty. Encouraged by his victory over Umma, Eannatum then proceeded to subdue other Sumerian city-states, among them Erech, Ur and Kish, so that for a brief period at

TO IRRIGATE THE FIELDS *of their parched plains, the Mesopotamians used sweeps like those shown working in tandem above—long poles counterweighted to raise buckets of water from the river and dump them into higher reservoirs. The reservoirs fed intricate systems of canals like the one below, drawn from a 1300 B.C. map of waterways and fields near Nippur. The main canal loops down around a U-shaped royal field at its bend, and is bordered by lands owned by temples or assigned to nearby villages (small round enclosures) and the citizens of Nippur.*

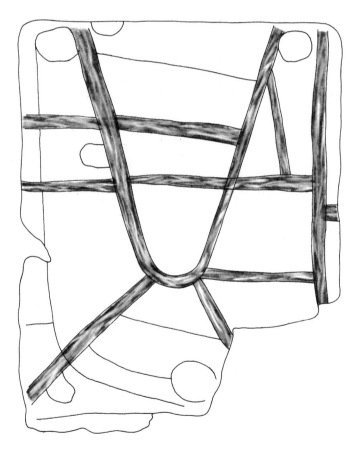

least Lagash could claim suzerainty over all Sumer. Eannatum's enemies gave him no respite, however. The proud "Prostrator of the Enemy Lands" was finally slain in battle, and thereafter the power of Lagash rapidly deteriorated.

Although eager to take advantage of Lagash's weakness, nearby Umma did not find a suitable opportunity to destroy its hated rival until several generations later, when a peace-loving, idealistic reformer named Urukagina ascended the Lagashite throne. Lugalzaggesi, a contentious and ambitious ruler of Umma, seized this moment to attack Lagash and burn and loot its temples. Though the city was largely ruined, a unique document of the luckless Urukagina survived; it is a moving record of the social reforms that protected the citizens of Lagash from bureaucratic injustice—in which the idea of the individual's freedom is expressed for the first time in man's written history.

Lugalzaggesi's triumph over Lagash was only the first in a series of victorious military campaigns. He soon made himself master of a number of Sumer's important cities, including its chief religious center of Nippur, moved his capital from Umma to Erech and in one of his inscriptions boasted that he controlled all the territory "from the Lower Sea [the Persian Gulf] to the Upper Sea [the Mediterranean]." But then came his turn to suffer the ignominies of defeat, and Lugalzaggesi ended his days in a neckstock at the gate of Nippur, target for the scorn and abuse of all who passed by.

His conqueror was the mighty Sargon, called the Great, one of the outstanding figures of the ancient world. A superb military leader, organizer and administrator, this extraordinary man became the first to weld Sumer and Mesopotamia's northern half into a single nation under one supreme authority, and the empire he carved out of Western Asia was to endure for nearly 200 years.

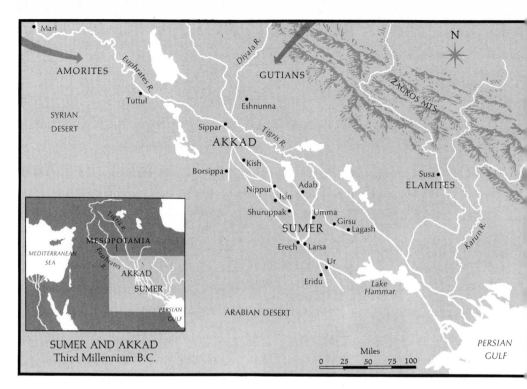

CLUSTERED CITIES, *built along the Tigris and Euphrates Rivers, marked the realms of Sumer and Akkad. At the end of the Third Millennium B.C., many of these cities were overrun by barbaric Amorites, Gutians and Elamites; Agade, the capital of Akkad, was so thoroughly demolished by Gutian invaders about 2200 B.C. that its ruins have yet to be discovered.*

Sargon was born around 2350 B.C., the son of Semites, the people who had begun to infiltrate Mesopotamia from the west in prehistoric Ubaidian times and who by now made up an appreciable part of the population. Little is known of his early life. According to a later, Moses-like legend, his mother entrusted the baby to fate by launching him on the Euphrates River in a pitch-covered basket. Fate was kind; a farmer drawing water to irrigate his field pulled the basket to safety and reared the child as his own.

When he reached manhood, Sargon became cupbearer to Ur-Zababa, the Sumerian king of Kish, but just how he rose from humble circumstances to this high office is unknown. Also unknown is the manner in which he managed to overthrow Ur-Zababa and claim his throne. Once in power, however, Sargon lost no time embarking on his phenomenal path of conquest, and most of his steps can be followed from surviving copies of his own contemporary inscriptions.

His first move was a surprise attack on Erech, Lugalzaggesi's capital, that resulted in the capture of its ruler and his imprisonment at Nippur. With Sumer's major political force thus eliminated, Sargon consolidated his hold on southern Mesopotamia by successfully hurling his phalanxes of lancers and archers and his ass-drawn war chariots against the minions of Lugalzaggesi, the cities of Ur, Umma and Lagash (which had recovered from its earlier destruction by Lugalzaggesi).

Sargon next subjugated the troublesome Elamites beyond Sumer's eastern boundary and led victorious military expeditions into northern Mesopotamia. Then he marched westward, extending his conquests as far as the Amanus and Taurus ranges near the Mediterranean coasts of Syria and Turkey. His armies may even have carried his might to such distant lands as Egypt, Ethiopia and India.

To maintain control over his vast realm, Sargon garrisoned its strategic outposts with Semitic troops and everywhere appointed fellow-Semites as his high administrative officials. Somewhere along the Euphrates in that part of south-central Mesopotamia then known as Akkad, he built a new capital for himself and called it Agade; although its precise location is unknown, the city is said to have been one of the most magnificent of antiquity, its temples and royal palace resplendent with treasures from all parts of the empire. From the land of Akkad came the name Akkadian given to the Semitic language that came into common use in Mesopotamia from Sargon's time onward. Akkadian is also the term by which modern scholars identify that period in Mesopotamian history dominated by Sargon and others of his line.

As is so often the case with mighty conquerors, Sargon's empire fell apart after his death. His two sons, faced with widespread revolts within Sumer and without, had their hands full trying to preserve even a part of their inheritance. His grandson Naram-Sin, to be sure, proved himself for a while a worthy successor to the great warrior-king. His conquests, too, ranged all over the ancient Near East, and his monument (now in the Louvre in Paris) commemorating a victory over the warlike Lullubi tribesmen of the Zagros Mountains epitomizes in eloquent stone his military prowess. On it the figure of Naram-Sin, armed with a bow and followed by his army, is seen trampling ruthlessly upon the bodies of fallen enemies while symbols of his protecting gods hover in the sky above.

But even the favorably disposed gods of Naram-Sin were helpless to avert the catastrophe that overwhelmed Sumer and its Semitic rulers in about 2200 B.C. The blow came in the form of an invasion by hordes of Gutians, fierce barbarians who poured down from the highlands to the northeast and wiped the splendid city of Agade from the face of the earth. Not only did the arrival of the Gutians spell doom for the dynasty founded by Sargon, but it also heralded the swift collapse of the great empire over which its kings had ruled.

Of all the Sumerian cities, Lagash alone seems to have flourished during the grim days that ensued, possibly because its governors were not above collaborating with the hated Gutians. One such governor, the prince Gudea, is perhaps the best-known figure of ancient Sumer; many statues of him have been unearthed among the city's ruins and most of them are now in museums. Some of the statues are inscribed with accounts of Gudea's ambitious building and rebuilding of Lagashite temples, and other contemporary inscriptions tell how he lavished upon these edifices a wealth of gold, silver and semiprecious stones.

Finally, after a century or so of brutal Gutian overlordship, a liberator of Sumer by the name of Utuhegal arose in Erech, the city that in earlier times had produced the heroic Gilgamesh and other great kings. Utuhegal campaigned against "the snake and scorpion of the mountain . . . who carried off the kingship of Sumer to the foreign land," crushed the Gutians and delivered his people from their oppressive yoke. But though brave and heroic, he was evidently not discriminating in his choice of subordinates. After reigning as supreme monarch of Sumer for only seven years, Utuhegal was deposed by Ur-Nammu, an ambitious general whom he had the poor judgment to appoint governor of Ur.

The line of kings that Ur-Nammu founded at Ur in approximately 2100 B.C. was the third in that city's history and the last Mesopotamian dynasty that could be termed Sumerian. During its century of dominance under Ur-Nammu and his descendants Sumer was restored to much of its former glory. Considerable portions of the empire lost since the time of Sargon and his heirs were reconquered; agriculture and commerce, which had largely fallen into stagnation under the barbaric Gutians, enjoyed a dramatic upswing; and in all branches of the arts there occurred a sudden and splendid renaissance.

Ur-Nammu, the usurper, turned out to be a strong and able king and an energetic builder throughout Sumer, especially at Ur. The remains of his ziggurat dedicated to the moon-god Nanna still stand there, an enduring monument to his memory. At its base this gigantic structure of brickwork covers an area of 200 by 140 feet; its original three terraced stages with their crowning shrine towered some 70 feet above the city. Ur-Nammu is also notable as the first known law-giver in history. His law code, parts of which have been found inscribed on cuneiform tablets, preceded the celebrated Code of Hammurabi of Babylon by more than three centuries and the laws of Moses by over a millennium.

Death seems to have come to Ur-Nammu on the battlefield fighting the Gutians, who despite their earlier defeat kept up their attacks against Sumer. His son Shulgi followed him on the throne and in the course of his 48-year reign proved to be one of the most brilliant and distinguished rulers of ancient Mesopotamia. The Sumerian poets of his day outdid themselves in composing hymns of exaltation and glorification in his honor, and apparently they did not exaggerate unduly in portraying him as a rare combination of sage, warrior, builder of temples, diplomat and lavish patron of the arts—a provider of all good things to his land and people.

It was during Shulgi's long reign and the reign of the king who succeeded him that the Sumerians regained control over a realm nearly as broad as Sargon's. But the curtain was about to descend upon Sumer and its great centuries. When Ibbi-Sin, fifth and last of Ur-Nammu's dynasty, came to the throne of Ur he found himself repelling major attacks on two fronts: by Sumer's old ene-my, the Elamites, in the east, and by a new foe who had arisen in the deserts of Syria and Arabia to the west, Semitic nomads known as Amorites.

Under these blows, Sumer and its empire began to disintegrate. Ibbi-Sin's generals and provincial governors, smelling doom in the air, threw off their loyalty to the monarch and each started to shift for himself. A key figure in the betrayal was one of the King's most trusted generals, Ishbi-Erra,

who not only managed to make himself master of Isin, a city some 80 miles northwest of Ur, but subverted the governors of other cities by means of force or threats. As a result Sumer was ruled for a time by two rival Kings—Ibbi-Sin at Ur and Ishbi-Erra at Isin.

This recurrence of Sumer's chronic disease—bitter internal conflict—added to ever-increasing pressure by enemies from without, drained the land of its strength. About 2000 B.C. the Elamites at-tacked and destroyed Ur and carried its King into a captivity from which he never returned. Although the city of Isin retained some prestige for a time, the fall of mighty Ur virtually marked the end of Sumer as a power. Before long Semitic Amorites drove the Elamites from the country, made Babylon their capital and submerged the Sumerians as an ethnic entity.

The calamity that had overtaken their land and cities made a deep impression on the poets of Sumer's final days. One of their lamentations may serve as a melancholy epitaph for the people who, more than 10 centuries earlier, first crossed the threshold of civilization and whose brilliant achieve-ments have enriched most of the great cultures since. It bemoans the day

That "law and order" cease to exist . . .
That cities be destroyed, that houses be destroyed . . .
That [Sumer's] rivers flow with bitter water . . .
That the mother care not for her children . . .
That kingship be carried off from the land . . .
That on the banks of the Tigris and Euphrates . . .
    there grow sickly plants . . .
That no one tread the highways, that no one seek
    out the roads,
That its well-founded cities and hamlets be
    counted as ruins,
That its teeming blackheaded people be put to
    the mace . . .
The fate decreed by [the gods] cannot be
    changed, who can overturn it!

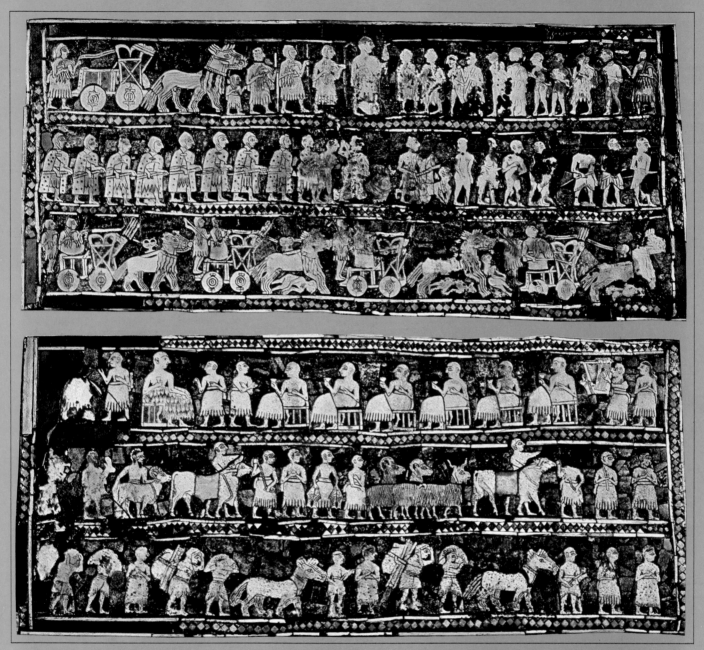

MEN FROM ALL WALKS OF LIFE *parade across the Standard of Ur. The top panel shows the Sumerians fighting a war; the bottom one, a procession to court.*

# THE PEOPLE OF SUMER

One of archeology's richest clues to life in ancient Sumer is a finely wrought wooden object known as the Standard of Ur *(above)*. Found in a 4,500-year-old grave in the city of Ur, its 18-inch-wide panels are inlaid in shell and lapis lazuli with a panorama of figures from all classes of society. One side shows soldiers in battle and leading prisoners to their king *(top row, center)*; the other depicts the king holding a banquet while commoners bring him gifts of livestock, produce and manufactured goods that formed the basis of Sumerian wealth and culture.

# A LAND OF FARMERS

Prosperity came to Mesopotamia, according to Sumerian legend, when the gods "made the ewe give birth to the lamb . . . [and] the grain increase in the furrows." The great majority of Sumerians, in fact, were farmers, and they produced the wealth that made civilization possible. The world's oldest agricultural manual is a Sumerian document that tells how to grow barley, Mesopotamia's staple food. Herdsmen raised pigs, goats and donkeys, as well as the cattle and sheep shown here in details from the Standard of Ur.   Oxen were used as draft animals, and their hides were tanned into leather. Sheep, which provided wool for a thriving textile industry, were so important that the Sumerians had 200 different words to describe various types.

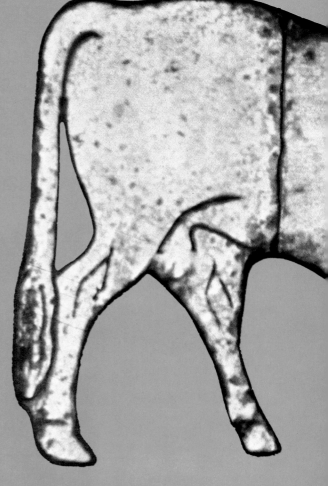

HEAVY-LADEN PORTERS, *each a detail from the Standard, convey produce probably traded in Sumerian markets. At left, a man carries a pack which may hav*

# A WEALTH OF TRADE

With the riches born of agriculture, a thriving trade
sprang up among the cities of Sumer and their
neighbors. Merchants led caravans laden with barley and textiles to Asia Minor and Iran, returning
with timber, stone and metals. Sumerian craftsmen
worked these raw materials into tools, weapons and
jewelry, further swelling the list of items for export.

*contained wool, while another man leads a ram. A bulging sack of grain or goods weighs down a third porter, while the man at right carries strings of fish.*

THE KING OF UR, *clad in a sheepskin skirt and holding a beaker of wine, sits on his throne and listens to a court harpist and singer (shown opposite).*

# THE LUXURY AND POWER OF THE COURT

To regulate trade and agriculture, each Sumerian state developed a powerful government, run by a class of bureaucrats and headed by a king. Though the king lived in luxury, attended by numerous retainers, his responsibilities were manifold. He built temples, administered justice and maintained the elaborate system of canals that irrigated the croplands. At first, Sumerian kings were elected. But in time the office became hereditary, and took on such an aura of pomp and legend that the Sumerians claimed their monarchs were appointed by heaven —and that the first one had reigned 28,800 years.

IN LINE OF BATTLE, *a row of infantrymen (top) levels short spears. The soldiers wear copper helmets and heavy protective cloaks studded with metal discs. In the*

# SOLDIERS OF THE KING

Waging war was one of the most important tasks of a Sumerian monarch. As conflicts arose between neighboring city-states over land and water rights, rulers raised large armies for defense. A specialized class of professional soldiers developed, meticulously drilled in the science of warfare; ranks of armored infantrymen attacked in disciplined formations (*left*) and wheeled chariots (*below*) decimated enemy lines. So effective were these professional warriors that their conquests encompassed all Mesopotamia, and helped carry the highly developed culture of the Sumerians far and wide.

*procession shown below them, a chariot with pegged wooden wheels and protected by a high armored shield is drawn by four donkeys led by a diminutive groom.*

# 3
# THE SWEEP OF EMPIRE

With the destruction of Ur around 2000 B.C. a millennium and a half of Sumerian dominance in Mesopotamia was drawing to a close. As a political power Sumer was soon eclipsed, but its rich cultural heritage lived on. It was taken over by new dynasties of kings founded by foreigners, and under their rule the Land Between the Rivers was to attain peaks of glory surpassing even those of Sumerian times.

During the 15 centuries that followed, these kings would consolidate Mesopotamia's city-states into new kingdoms governed from splendid new capitals, and two of the kingdoms—Babylonia in the region's southern half and Assyria in the north—would grow into mighty empires. Each in its turn would know periods of power followed by eras of decline and domination by the other, and brilliant resurgence. Before their ultimate downfall each would spread its influence, culturally and by force of arms, throughout vast tracts of the ancient Near Eastern world.

For some hundreds of years following the end of the Sumerian age, most of the rulers who shaped Mesopotamian history were Amorites or descendants of Amorites, Semites of the Syrian and Arabian deserts. Incursions by these nomads from the west, coupled with the Elamite attacks from what is now Iran, had caused Sumer to totter at the end of the Third Millennium B.C., but this was not the first time Amorites had appeared in the region. Wild and barbarous tribesmen who lived mainly by cattle-raising and sheepherding, they had for a number of years looked toward civilized Mesopotamia with envious eyes and during this period they had been infiltrating the land as peaceful workers and as mercenaries in Sumerian armies.

Finally, with the weakening of Sumer that followed the Elamites' destruction of Ur, the desert Amorites saw their opportunity to exchange their tents and barren grazing grounds for the cities and fertile farmlands of the Tigris-Euphrates plain. Overflowing the wall of fortresses built to keep them in check, they poured into Mesopotamia in conquering waves and occupied one Sumerian center after another. Nor was it long before many of these Amorite nomads had become fully urbanized, adopting from their Sumerian predecessors much of their religion, literature, law and art. They did, however, retain their Semitic tongue for their speech and documents, and Sumerian was relegated to the schools and temples, where it was studied, spoken and written until the time of Christ.

One of the Sumerian centers conquered by the invaders was Babylon, an unimportant town about 50 miles south of present-day Baghdad, and here a sheikh named Sumuabum founded an Amorite dynasty in 1850 B.C. Under Hammurabi, sixth of Sumuabum's line and one of the most celebrated rulers of the ancient Near East, Babylon was to win suzerainty over all Mesopotamia and give its name to the land once known as Sumer.

When Hammurabi ascended the Babylonian throne in 1750 B.C., Mesopotamia was still fragmented into the pattern of rival city-states that had reasserted itself shortly before the fall of Ur and its empire two centuries earlier. Many of the cities, to be sure, were now ruled by Hammurabi's fellow-Amorites. But their bond of blood had not brought about enduring peace, and the region continued to be torn by warfare as the center of power shifted from one city to another. Thus it was that Hammurabi found himself inheriting a state ringed about by ambitious and aggressive rivals. The most prominent of these were Larsa, dominating the cities to the south, Mari to the northwest in Syria, Eshnunna to the north and Assur—the city from which Assyria derived its name—about 200 miles northwest of Babylon on the banks of the Tigris.

The new King of Babylon was not content merely to maintain an uneasy coexistence with his dangerous neighbors. Driven by a desire to mold a deeply divided land into a unified state that—like its precursor, Sumer—would play a prominent role in the ancient world, Hammurabi proceeded to overwhelm and destroy his rivals one by one. At the beginning of his reign Babylon could lay claim

to a territory less than 50 miles in radius; when he died 42 years later his city was the capital of a realm reaching from the Persian Gulf to beyond the border of modern Turkey and from the Zagros ranges in the east to the Khabur River in Syria. All this Hammurabi achieved by a remarkable combination of statesmanship, cunning and courage; he understood when to bide his time, when to give and bend and when to strike.

In fact, Hammurabi restrained himself for more than a quarter of a century. Those years were spent in reinforcing his position, mostly by entering into political or military alliances that he did not hesitate to break whenever it suited his drive for power. At length he felt strong enough to launch a series of all-out attacks against his major rivals. In the 31st year of his reign he suddenly assaulted and took the city of Larsa, emerging from the battle as master of southern and central Mesopotamia.

Three years later he seized control of western Mesopotamia by crushing Mari, with which he had once been allied, leaving it in ruins. In our own time French archeologists have excavated at the site of Mari, and in the remains of its huge royal palace they have uncovered archives consisting of more than 20,000 clay tablets, including hundreds of official letters that date from the reign of Hammurabi. The contents of the letters have shed much light on this turbulent period of Mesopotamian history; they have also resulted in a reassessment of the importance of some of its major figures, Hammurabi among them.

Scholars once thought of this Babylonian King as the overriding monarch of his time, a judgment based largely on his famous Law Code, which was believed to be the world's oldest before the discovery of Sumerian forerunners. Great was the modern investigators' surprise to read in the Mari records that Hammurabi's contemporaries had not always viewed him so. One letter points out that before his victory over Larsa—the first significant step on his road to empire—Hammurabi was looked upon as just one of several Near Eastern kings of about equal power: "There is no king who is mighty by himself. Ten or fifteen kings follow Hammurabi, the man of Babylon, a like number Rim-Sin of Larsa, a like number Ibalpiel of Eshnunna . . . and twenty follow Yarimlim of Yamkhad [a Syrian state in the region of Aleppo]."

Although his contemporaries may not have been impressed with Hammurabi's stature at the outset of his conquests, there was no denying his might once he had brought southern, central and western Mesopotamia under his rule. Now it was time to complete his domination of the entire region. This he accomplished by overwhelming Eshnunna, a city about 65 miles north of Babylon that, in league with the chief Assyrian city of Assur, held sway over much of Mesopotamia's north. With the capture and sacking of Eshnunna, Hammurabi also gained at least nominal control over Assyria.

Hammurabi was now at the peak of his career, lord of a unified domain that included virtually all of Mesopotamia and its environs. In the prologue to his Law Code—the best-known copy of which is engraved on a stele, or stone shaft, preserved in the Louvre in Paris—he boasted that Babylon was now "supreme in the world" and that the foundations of his kingship were "as firm as those of heaven and earth." According to this same prologue, it was the gods who had instructed him "to make justice appear in the land, to destroy the evil and the wicked that the strong might not oppress the weak, to rise like the sun-god . . . to give light to the land."

Considerable information has survived about Hammurabi's administration of his empire. In addition to his detailed legal code, there exist a number of his letters to Babylonians appointed as officials in conquered provinces. The correspondence reveals that this extraordinary man was not only a formidable warrior and an astute diplomat but also a diligent, meticulous manager with a sincere interest in the well-being of his subjects. His letters show that he devoted as much personal attention to such minor matters as the payment of rents and petty lawsuits as he did to tax collecting and the maintenance of Babylonia's all-important irrigation systems.

By and large, however, Hammurabi's reign—while it unified and enlightened the land—made little alteration in Mesopotamia's fundamental way of life. Since Babylonia now controlled all the trade routes crisscrossing the region as well as the rich farmlands to the south, material prosperity no doubt increased—at least within Babylonia itself—but culturally there was hardly any break with the past. Most of the gods of Sumerian days, although given Semitic names, continued to be worshiped according to time-honored traditions. (Marduk, the god of Babylon, eventually replaced the Sumerian deity Enlil at the head of the pantheon, but this probably occurred after Hammurabi's reign.) In literature, the old myths and legends persisted with only slight variations, and the art and architecture of the period show no striking changes or innovations.

The kingship whose foundations were "as firm as those of heaven and earth" did not long survive its architect. Hammurabi died about 1708 B.C., after enjoying the fruits of success for only a few years, and almost immediately his empire began to fall apart. Revolts flared up everywhere. Although Hammurabi's son made valiant attempts to hold his inheritance together, Babylonia's northern and southern provinces were soon lost and the realm shrank to a small territory around the capital city. Others of Hammurabi's line continued to rule in Babylon for more than a century, but most of these rulers concentrated on domestic matters rather than on conquests beyond their borders.

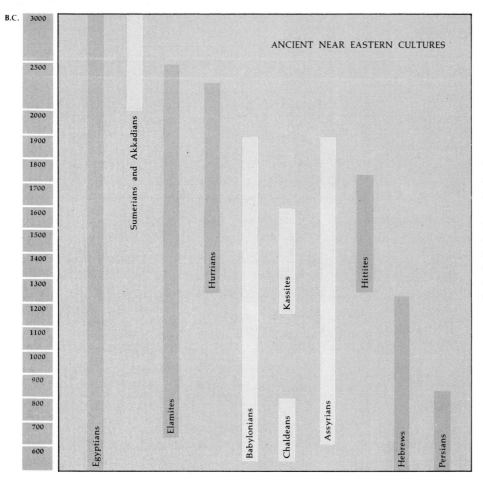

3000
2500
2000
1900
1800
1700
1600
1500
1400
1300
1200
1100
1000
900
800
700
600

ANCIENT NEAR EASTERN CULTURES

Sumerians and Akkadians

Hurrians

Kassites

Hittites

Egyptians

Elamites

Babylonians

Chaldeans

Assyrians

Hebrews

Persians

THE PROMINENT CULTURES *of the ancient Near East are listed in a chronological chart to show the centuries in which they flourished. The gold bars represent the cultures of Mesopotamia proper: Sumerian and Akkadian, Babylonian and Assyrian, which originated in the area, and Kassite and Chaldean, which were brought in by invaders. All these civilizations markedly influenced the cultures of the neighboring peoples, indicated in gray.*

Then, around 1600 B.C., the dynasty of the great Hammurabi came to an inglorious end. Its downfall was caused by a brief but destructive invasion by Hittites, a people from Anatolia (Asia Minor) who several centuries later were to become a major power in the Near East. The Hittites raided Babylonia, plundered Babylon, then withdrew to their homeland. Drained of its last strength by this disaster, the land was now fair prey to anyone interested in conquest—and conquerors quickly appeared. They were Kassites, non-Semitic invaders from the Zagros Mountains to the east, and they ruled Babylonia for the next four and a quarter centuries.

The Kassite occupation of Babylonia coincided with an age when the political structure of the entire Near East was undergoing momentous changes. In the lands neighboring on Mesopotamia new and vigorous nations had come into being, and still others were in the process of formation. Also, along the eastern coast of the Mediterranean, cities founded by Semitic peoples were increasing in importance. Thus in Kassite Babylonian times the Near

East was becoming a more and more complex place; as the area became more settled the future history of Mesopotamia was to be ever more closely linked with that of other lands.

A few generations after gaining control of Babylonia the Kassites had become fully Babylonian in literature, religion and general way of life and had given up their native language for the Semitic tongue of their subjects. Under their rule, order and prosperity returned to the land. New towns were built; the temples at Nippur, Ur and other ancient cities, neglected since the Hittite disaster, were restored and embellished; the provinces of southern Mesopotamia lost by Hammurabi's son were won back. For a while the Kassite kings, mindful of the days of Hammurabi when northern Mesopotamia acknowledged Babylonian overlordship, also laid claim to Assyria.

Curiously, modern scholars know about this not from documents found on Mesopotamian soil, but from letters of the 14th Century B.C. discovered in far-off Egypt. Part of an archive of diplomatic correspondence, the letters were unearthed in 1887 at Tell el-Amarna, site of Egypt's capital in the reign of Akhenaton, the heretic pharaoh who attempted to replace the multiple Egyptian gods with a single universal deity. Among the letters written to the pharaoh in cuneiform characters and in Akkadian, then the *lingua franca* of the ancient world, were two from Assuruballit, an Assyrian king. They dealt primarily with nothing more momentous than an exchange of gifts between the two monarchs. But there was also a letter from Burnaburiash, the Kassite king of Babylonia who was Assuruballit's contemporary. Outraged at the presumption of the Assyrian ruler in sending envoys to the pharaoh, Burnaburiash demanded that they be sent home empty-handed from Egypt since Babylonia considered Assyria its vassal.

The Assyrians viewed things differently. In the mid-14th Century B.C., the time of Burnaburiash's complaint to the Egyptian throne, they had just recovered from some 400 years of adversity and had no intention of admitting subservience to Babylonia. They had once wielded impressive power in their own right, and they hoped for a return to this former might.

Assyria's first period as a power to be reckoned with had occurred shortly before the reign of Hammurabi when Shamshi-Adad, a brilliant Amorite ruler, led its armies to domination over most of northern Mesopotamia. But with the death of this warrior-king, Assyria's authority declined and in order to survive the Assyrians had become dependent on their alliance with the city of Eshnunna. When Eshnunna fell to Hammurabi the Assyrians, too, were forced to accept Babylonian rule.

After Hammurabi died and his empire crumbled, Assyria fell upon even more dismal times. For two and a half centuries it lived in the dread shadow of the Hurrians—the Old Testament Horites—a crude and warlike people from the region of Lake Van in mountainous Armenia who gradually settled all over northern Mesopotamia and Syria. The Hurrians' military might stemmed chiefly from their use of chariots drawn by horses, animals that may have been introduced into Western Asia from the plains of southern Russia. By about 1500 B.C. the Hurrians had established a dominant centralized state known as Mitanni, and Assyria became one of its vassals. Mitanni's strength lasted only a century or so; it began to wane as the Hittite empire arose and extended its power well beyond the bounds of Anatolia. This gave Assyria an opportunity to regain its independence, which it did in about 1350 B.C. under the same Assuruballit who traded gifts with Akhenaton of Egypt.

Toward the end of his reign Assuruballit made it evident that Kassite Babylonia would have to consider Assyria an equal rather than a subject state. By then he wielded considerable influence and through adroit political maneuvering managed to place his part-Assyrian, part-Babylonian grandson, Kurigalzu, on the Babylonian throne—but with results he had not foreseen. Once installed as king, Kurigalzu became a true patriot of Babylonia and a determined protector of its interests. To bolster his defenses he founded an important new fortified city called Dur-Kurigalzu, the modern Aqarquf, near Baghdad. The remains of the city's huge ziggurat, rising to a height of some 170 feet, still overshadow the surrounding plain; more than one early European traveler mistook them for the ruins of the Tower of Babel and thus identified Aqarquf as the site of ancient Babylon.

Since Babylonia's political interests conflicted with those of its newly independent and power-hungry neighbor, it was not long before Kurigalzu became embroiled in a war with Assyria, now ruled by his own blood relative, Assuruballit's son. The outcome of this struggle was inconclusive and the two kingdoms established their frontiers by treaty, but thereafter the balance of power seems to have swung in favor of Assyria. One Assyrian monarch, Tukulti-Ninurta, actually brought Babylonia under his rule for a while, capturing its Kassite king and boasting in an inscription that "on his royal neck I trod with my foot as on a footstool."

It was not the Assyrians, however, who ultimately toppled Babylonia's long-lasting Kassite dynasty. The death blow for the Kassites came from the East. Around 1170 B.C. southern Mesopotamia's old enemies, the Elamites of Iran, after centuries of nonaggression, invaded Babylonia, overthrew its last Kassite king and plundered its cities. Among the spoils of war they carried back to Elam were such national treasures as the famous stele inscribed with Hammurabi's Law Code and—most humiliating of all—the statue of Babylonia's chief deity, Marduk.

With the astonishing resilience that had characterized the Mesopotamians since early Sumerian times, the Babylonians quickly rallied from this disaster and under a new native dynasty regained some of their prestige and power. One of their rulers, Nebuchadrezzar I, expelled the garrisons left by the Elamites, attacked Elam itself and brought Marduk's statue back to its temple in Babylon. About 1100 B.C. another Babylonian king went so far as to invade Assyria, penetrating to within 20 miles of Assur, its capital, before his army was routed.

But the balance of power had by now shifted decisively in favor of the Assyrians. Around the beginning of the 11th Century B.C. Babylonia entered an era of political decline from which it would not fully recover for another 400 years or so. The fortunes of Assyria, on the other hand, soared spectacularly. By nature more belligerent than the Babylonians—who placed greater emphasis on cultural achievement than they did on warfare—the Assyrians about this time embarked upon a pol-

icy of ruthless conquest that would ultimately make them masters over nearly all the Near East. But their climb to power was not to be a smooth ascent. Interrupting it would be several periods when Assyria's fortunes sank to a low ebb and the Assyrian star seemed in danger of total eclipse.

The monarch who played the outstanding part in leading Assyria to its first new era of prominence was Tiglath-Pileser I. This king began his reign by vanquishing an Anatolian horde that threatened the city of Nineveh north of Assur as well as Assyria's vital trade routes from Asia Minor, main source of the iron by then in use in most of the civilized ancient world. Later, to secure his northern and eastern frontiers, he subdued the aggressive tribes around and beyond Lake Van in Armenia and the fierce mountaineers of the Zagros ranges. In the west he marched his army across Syria all the way to the Mediterranean coast, where he exacted tribute from the wealthy Phoenician cities of Byblos, Sidon and Arvad. Also in the west, Tiglath-Pileser forced back across the Euphrates tribes of Semitic nomads known as Aramaeans who for some time had been encroaching on Mesopotamian territory. Finally he struck south and captured Babylon, an ephemeral victory since he failed to follow it up with any substantial control of the land and its people.

Tiglath-Pileser's successes on the battlefield were matched by the benefits he conferred upon his homeland. His conquests had brought unprecedented prosperity to Assyria, enabling him to carry out large-scale rehabilitation programs. He restored the ziggurats and the principal temple of Assur, his capital; he reroofed the temple with cedar obtained as tribute from cities on the coasts of Syria and Lebanon, and installed in it a library of literary works. At Nineveh, he laid out attractive new parks and diverted the waters from a tributary of the nearby Tigris to irrigate them.

Similar beautifying projects were undertaken at other Assyrian centers and many agricultural reforms were instituted during his kingship, so that Tiglath-Pileser had reason to boast that he had served his people well, and "in peaceful habitations . . . caused them to dwell."

Paradoxically, it was this same restorer of temples and cities who was instrumental in developing the policy of cruelty and butchery that would make later Assyrian kings dreaded throughout the ancient world. All wars are cruel, but from Tiglath-Pileser onward the Assyrians placed an emphasis on terror and torture that is well-nigh unique in the history of literate, civilized peoples. Much of their ferocity and belligerence resulted from Assyria's geographical position; it was surrounded by enemies who ever threatened its existence. But a good deal of Assyria's dependence on sheer physical power and brutality also stemmed no doubt from a feeling of cultural inferiority to neighboring Babylonia, from which it had borrowed writing, literature and many religious, economic and legal ideas and practices.

Inscriptions commemorating Tiglath-Pileser's military triumphs set the pattern followed and elaborated upon by all later Assyrian rulers. They abound with gory accounts of Assyria's policy of terror in operation. Typical of Tiglath-Pileser's inscriptions is his account of his victories over the Anatolians and their allies endangering the region north of Nineveh: "With their twenty thousand warriors and their five kings I fought . . . and I defeated them. . . . Their blood I let flow in the valleys and on the high levels of the mountains. I cut off their heads and outside their cities, like heaps of grain, I piled them up . . . I burned their cities with fire, I demolished them, I cleared them away. . . ."

But submission gained through terror does not breed loyalty. Tiglath-Pileser had not been a good colonial administrator; content to rule by fear alone, he had failed to consolidate his realm by setting up a strong administration in the conquered territories. Upon his death, in about 1080 B.C., the suppressed people rose in revolt, quickly shattering his far-flung domain. For the next century and a half Assyria—and much of the rest of Mesopotamia as well—knew some of its darkest days. Pressed by the nomadic Aramaean tribes to the west and harassed by the Zagros mountaineers to the east, the Assyrians were gradually squeezed into a strip along the Tigris barely 100 miles long and 50 miles wide. In Babylonia as well, the Aramaeans overran the land. One of their tribes, the Kaldu, settled near the head of the Persian Gulf; from them comes the name Chaldea, often used by ancient Greek and Hebrew writers to designate Babylonia.

Assyria's phenomenal emergence from 150 years of hard times to become one of the mightiest military powers of antiquity began toward the end of the 10th Century B.C. Under a King named Adadnirari II the land was liberated from the pressures that confined it. First the Aramaeans were driven from the Tigris valley; then Adadnirari lashed out at the peoples of the Zagros Mountains, cutting them down "in heaps"; later he wrested considerable territory from northern Babylonia. His son, Tukulti-Ninurta II, also acquired territory, and by his death Assyria had grown from a sadly shrunken state beside the Tigris into a kingdom that embraced much of Mesopotamia's north.

The first truly illustrious ruler of newly arisen Assyria was the son of Tukulti-Ninurta II, Assurnasirpal II. Along with the kingship this ruler inherited the best soldiers in the Near East, trained and hardened by years of rigorous campaigning and organized into corps of swift horse-drawn chariotry, cavalry, bowmen and lancers. In addition to these units there were engineers equipped with iron-headed battering rams and other siege weapons.

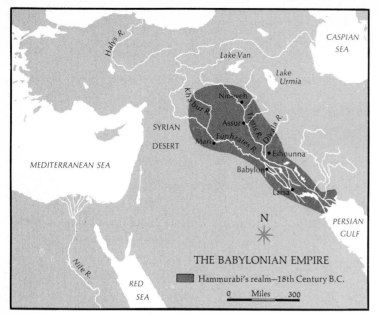

A SHORT-LIVED POWER, *the Babylonian empire reached its peak during the reign of its founder, Hammurabi. It declined after Hammurabi's death, but its capital, Babylon, remained a great cultural center for more than a thousand years.*

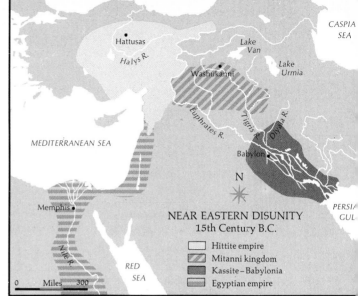

HOSTILE STATES *battled to control Mesopotamia in the centuries following Babylonia's decline. An alliance between Egypt and Mitanni checked Hittite expansion southward. Kassite invaders from the east ruled Babylonia.*

As Tiglath-Pileser I had done almost two centuries earlier, Assurnasirpal II carried Assyria's arms far beyond the limits of Mesopotamia to the shores of the Mediterranean. He washed his weapons in the sea to symbolize his domination over the Phoenician cities, then marched homeward across Syria laden with tribute—gold, silver, tin, copper, ivory, rare woods and exotic animals. Most of Assurnasirpal's campaigns, however, were more in the nature of forays in search of plunder; on the whole he acquired little new territory. But he succeeded in making Assyria a name that struck panic into the hearts of its neighbors. His coldly objective recording of atrocities presents a baleful picture: "I built a pillar over against his city gate, and I flayed all the chief men . . . and I covered the pillar with their skins; some I walled up within the pillar, some I impaled upon the pillar on stakes . . . and I cut off the limbs of the officers. . . ." And again: "Many captives from among them I burned with fire. . . From some I cut off their hands and their fingers, and from others I cut off their noses, their ears . . . of many I put out the eyes. . . . Their young men and maidens I burned in the fire. . . ."

And yet this pitiless despot could be creative as well as destructive, especially in relation to his own land. About 20 miles south of modern Mosul he

built a magnificent new capital, Calah (present-day Nimrud), settled it with peoples captured during his campaigns and carried out large irrigation projects in the surrounding countryside. At Calah he resided in a six-acre palace, a richly decorated labyrinth of ceremonial halls, royal apartments, storerooms and airy courts. According to Assurnasirpal's own description of it, substantiated by archeological excavations, it must have been a sumptuous edifice indeed:

"A palace of cedar, cypress, juniper, boxwood, mulberry, pistachio-wood, and tamarisk, for my royal dwelling and for my lordly pleasure for all time I founded therein. Beasts of the mountains and of the seas of white limestone and alabaster I fashioned, and set them up in its gates. I made it suitable, I made it glorious. . . . Door-leaves of cedar, cypress, juniper, and mulberry I hung in the gates thereof; and silver, gold, tin, bronze and iron, the spoil of my hand from the lands which I had brought under my sway, in great quantities I took and I placed therein."

An inscription unearthed at Calah describing in detail the immense banquet given by the king to celebrate the completion of his royal city indicates that he was as lavish with his entertainment as he was ruthless in war. For ten days 69,574

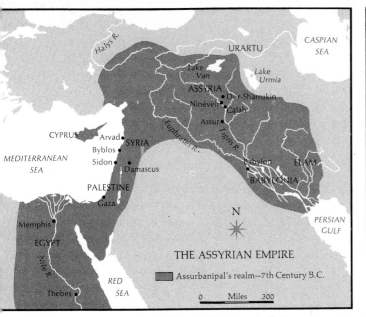

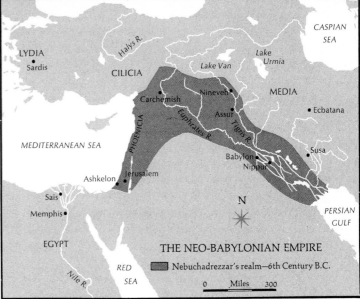

WARLIKE ASSYRIA, once part of the Mitanni kingdom, built its own empire through conquest. Its mightiest king, Assurbanipal, ruled a vast crescent-shaped area from Egypt to the Persian Gulf from his capital at Nineveh.

THE LAST GREAT POWER in Mesopotamia, the empire of Nebuchadrezzar II arose in Babylonia after the break-up of the Assyrian empire at the end of the Seventh Century B.C. It lasted until 539 B.C., when Babylon fell to the Persians.

guests from his new capital and from all corners of his realm feasted on 2,200 oxen and 16,000 sheep, as well as large and small birds, gazelles, fish, eggs and huge quantities of wine and beer. The inscription ends on a note oddly at variance with what one might expect of a rapacious sanguinary monarch; Assurnasirpal rejoices in having regaled the inhabitants of Calah and "the happy people of all the lands," and in having sent them back to their homes "in peace and joy."

Assurnasirpal's son, Shalmaneser III, spread the terror of Assyria's name even more widely than his father had done. After ascending the throne in 858 B.C., he spent virtually all of his 35-year reign on the battlefield. His military campaigns, many of them plundering expeditions like his father's, ranged from the mountains of Armenia to the head of the Persian Gulf and from the Zagros ranges westward to Cilicia in Asia Minor. In Palestine, where the Hebrews had founded the kingdom of Israel around 1000 B.C., the Israelite King Jehu prostrated himself before Shalmaneser and added Israel's tribute to that wrung from Phoenician princes.

Not everywhere was Shalmaneser victorious, however. He failed to conquer the Aramaean city-state of Damascus in Syria, for example, and he nev-

er obtained more than nominal authority over Babylonia. A court rebellion leading to civil strife marked the end of his kingship and the beginning of some 75 years of Assyrian decline. Plagued with internal unrest, unrelenting pressure from aggressor states and some serious defeats, Assyria gradually lost control of most of the territories it had overrun.

But in the middle of the Eighth Century B.C. under Tiglath-Pileser III—called Pul in the Old Testament—the Assyrian juggernaut began rolling again with renewed might and fury—and it continued to roll for more than a hundred years. Before it stopped it crushed virtually all the Near Eastern peoples and created the greatest empire the world had yet known.

The framework of empire established by Tiglath-Pileser III was to prevail with little change until Assyria's ultimate eclipse. Under him, wars ceased to be primarily campaigns to amass as much booty as possible and became enduring conquests. He regained control over all former territories, and most of these—as well as many of his new acquisitions—became Assyrian provinces. Governing each province was a strong and efficient administration composed of Assyrian officials directly responsible to the king and charged with such duties as preserving law and order, building public works and collecting taxes. Revolts, which were to become so common in later imperial days that they ultimately destroyed the empire, were harshly suppressed; the entire population of a potentially troublesome city or district was often deported to a far-distant region and the vacancy filled by other conquered people. A system of messenger relay stations enabled Tiglath-Pileser III to be in constant communication with all parts of his realm. In the courts of satellite nations his representatives kept an ever watchful eye on all matters pertaining to Assyria's interests, including an uninterrupted flow of tribute.

Under Tiglath-Pileser III there also began the reorganization of the Assyrian army that transformed it into the most formidable military machine of its day. Previously the army had been called up for the duration of a campaign or a national emergency, and, since it was composed mainly of the peasantry of Assyria proper, it was limited in size. Now, as Assyria began to expand, the army became a large standing force whose core was still Assyrian but whose ranks were swelled by foreign mercenaries and contingents of troops from vassal states and soldiers levied in annexed provinces.

Riding in his war chariot at the head of his newly reorganized army, Tiglath-Pileser III outdid all of his predecessors in extending Assyria's power. Besides thrusting deeper into what is today Iran than any previous Assyrian king, he claimed vast new areas in Asia Minor, consolidated Assyria's position in much of Syria by conquering the city of Damascus, and strengthened his authority along the eastern Mediterranean seaboard. One of his Mediterranean expeditions swept as far as Gaza, near the Egyptian frontier. Closer to home, Tiglath-Pileser III overthrew a Chaldean sheikh who had usurped the Babylonian throne and in so doing became the first Assyrian monarch to impose his kingship effectively on that land in more than 450 years—since Tukulti-Ninurta had captured one of

its Kassite kings and trod upon his royal neck.

Until the Assyrians threatened Gaza, Egyptian-Assyrian relations had been generally amicable. But facing the specter of Assyrian arms at its door-step—as well as a mounting Assyrian interference in Egyptian trade with the rich cities of Phoenicia —Egypt began to have second thoughts about its relations with Assyria. To counter the combined military and economic threat, Egypt began to incite uprisings among Assyria's vassals in Palestine and Syria, even going so far as to lend them large bodies of troops. At the same time the Assyrians were having trouble with the people of Urartu, a powerful though relatively youthful nation in Armenia that for years had been stirring up unrest in the subject provinces.

Thus, when a king called Sargon—a name made famous 16 centuries before by Sargon of Akkad— came to rule Assyria in 721 B.C., he found himself heir to an empire aflame with revolt. Compounding his problems was the fact that early in his reign another Chaldean leader, supported by the Elamites, seized mastery of Babylonia and renounced Assyrian control. Like his predecessors, Sargon II made considerable additions to the Assyrian empire, but he spent as much time stamping out revolutions, crushing the armies of their instigators and rewinning former territories, including Babylonia, as he did in making new conquests.

Toward the end of his reign Sargon II decided to move his capital from Calah to a new site called Dur-Sharrukin (modern Khorsabad) near Nineveh. Within 10 years he raised there a great new city whose palace rivaled in glory that of Assurnasirpal at Calah. Standing guard at its gates were enormous stone figures with the bodies of bulls and human heads, and nearly a mile and a half of alabaster and limestone reliefs adorned its walls. But Sargon did not long enjoy his new capital; soon after it was completed he was slain in battle.

The death of Sargon II was the signal for a new wave of uprisings in various parts of the empire. Especially serious were those in Palestine and Phoenicia, where a number of subject cities had entered into dangerous new alliances with Egypt, and in Babylonia, once again dominated by a truculent Chaldean.

Although Sargon's son and successor, the famous Sennacherib, is notable for making Nineveh one of the most splendid capitals of antiquity, he is probably best remembered in history for the manner in which he dealt with the insurgents in Palestine and Babylonia. His own annals, somewhat paralleling the Biblical account of the event in the Second Book of Kings, tell how his army stormed into Palestine, capturing 46 fortified cities and seizing 200,150 people as spoils of war. Jerusalem, capital of Judah (the southern part of the kingdom of Israel) and a principal seat of rebellion, was besieged, and Hezekiah, its king, was forced into submission. The Assyrians spared the city—but for this Hezekiah paid a staggering price. In Sennacherib's words: "To his former annual tribute I added further tribute and presents due to my majesty. . . . He sent [a convoy] after me to Nineveh, my royal city, with 30 talents of gold, 800 talents of silver, jewels, antimony . . . couches of ivory, easy chairs inlaid with ivory, elephants' hides, elephants' tusks . . . all kinds of valuable treasures, and his daughters, his harem, and male and female singers. . . ."

Sennacherib's revenge on Babylon was far more savage. Previous Assyrian rulers, aware of their cultural indebtedness to Babylonia, had treated the city with deference, but Sennacherib destroyed it utterly: "With [the corpses of its inhabitants] I filled the city squares. . . . The city and houses, from its foundation to its top, I destroyed, I devastated, I burned with fire. The wall and outer wall, temples and gods, temple-towers of brick and

earth, as many as there were, I razed. . . . Through the midst of that city I dug canals [from the Euphrates River], I flooded its site with water. . . . That in days to come the site of that city, and [its] temples and gods, might not be recognized, I dissolved it in water, . . . annihilated it, making it like a meadow." But the gods whose temples Sennacherib had razed could also be vindictive; the fate they decreed for him was murder. Eight years after destroying Babylon he was brutally killed by his own sons.

It was not one of Sennacherib's assassins, however, who now came to power. After a brief period of dynastic struggle, another son, Esarhaddon, seized the throne and in his brief reign of 11 years proved to be one of the most remarkable of all Assyrian monarchs. Besides rebuilding Babylon, which for a decade had lain in ruins, Esarhaddon managed through arms and diplomacy not only to neutralize the principal foes on Assyria's borders but also to bring a period of peace to most of the lands under his rule. With his empire relatively quiet and his frontiers made secure, he was prepared to carry the power and terror of Assyria to another continent. In 671 B.C. he launched the invasion of Egypt.

It took Esarhaddon less than a month to overwhelm Egypt, once the proudest of nations, with a civilization almost as old as Mesopotamia's. But Egypt had grown feeble with age; although still influential enough politically to fan revolt among Assyria's vassals and assist them with troops, it lacked the strength to halt the advance of Esarhaddon's army. The northern Egyptian capital of Memphis fell after a siege of only a day and a half, and for about 16 years Egypt was merely another Assyrian province.

Assyria was now at the zenith of its glory and Esarhaddon could well boast: "I am powerful, I am all-powerful. . . . I am without an equal among all kings." The empire that he bequeathed to his successor, Assurbanipal, was immense, stretching from the Valley of the Nile in Egypt almost as far as the Caucasus Mountains in Armenia, a distance of more than 1,000 miles. Enriching the cities, palaces and temples of the heartland along the Tigris was a steady stream of tribute exacted from the far-flung provinces and from satellite kings—gold and ivory from Egypt, iron for weapons from Asia Minor, silver mined in the Amanus Mountains of northwestern Syria, lapis lazuli and other precious stones from Iran, valuable timber cut in the forests of Lebanon, rare plants and animals from all corners of the empire to stock the royal botanical gardens and zoos. To all appearances Assyria under Assurbanipal was indeed the most powerful nation in the world.

But time was running out for the warrior kings who had vanquished and terrorized nearly all the lands and peoples of the Near East. Their conquests had been so widespread that they were now overextended; it was impossible for Assyria to defend its many frontiers and at the same time to quell rebellions in the provinces. Beginning in Assurbanipal's reign, hatred of Assyrian cruelty and rapacity erupted in a series of massive revolts throughout the empire—and after him there was no king strong enough to stamp them out. When, toward the end of the Seventh Century B.C., a young and hitherto little heard of people—the Medes of the Iranian plateau—joined forces with the Chaldeans of Babylonia, they soon succeeded in toppling Assyria and laying waste Nineveh, Assur and many other of its cities. The Assyrian giant was dead and gone, and there was no one to shed a tear.

For the next 75 years a line of Chaldean kings enthroned in Babylon held mastery over Mesopotamia. Under them Babylonia enjoyed a brilliant resurgence—a burst of power and glory reminiscent of the age of Hammurabi more than 1,000 years earlier. The towering monarch of this so-called Neo-Babylonian empire was Nebuchadrezzar II. In re-establishing Mesopotamian control over western territories lost in the debacle of Assyria's collapse—Palestine, Syria and the rich trading cities of the Phoenician coast—he displayed almost as much ferocity as any Assyrian warlord. It was he who razed Jerusalem in 586 B.C., burned the Temple of Solomon and exiled the Jews to Babylonia. But it was also Nebuchadrezzar who beautified Babylon and made it the cosmopolitan as well as the cultural center of his day. Dominating the renovated city was the fabulous Tower of Babel, a colossal ziggurat rising to a height of almost 300 feet; the city's gates, palaces and temples glittered with glazed brickwork in red, cream, blue and yellow; the artificial "hanging gardens" built by Nebuchadrezzar were so impressive that they were regarded as one of the wonders of the ancient world.

Babylonia's renaissance was as short-lived as it was splendid. The rulers who followed Nebuchadrezzar were weak and vacillating. Nabonidus, the last king of Babylonia, incurred the wrath of many of his compatriots by attempting to substitute another deity for the supreme god Marduk, and the religious dissension he stirred up helped to ease the way for a conqueror with a reputation for respecting the traditions of those he subjected. That conqueror was Cyrus, King of the Persians, a people who had become the predominant power in Iran by the middle of the Sixth Century B.C. A brilliant warrior and an outstanding statesman, Cyrus had already carved out for himself an enormous realm that reached from India to Lydia on the Aegean coast of Asia Minor. In the autumn of 539 B.C. he took Babylon with hardly a fight, and the Cradle of Civilization, now time-worn and battered, became part of the Persian empire.

DECKED OUT FOR THE HUNT, *with flowered tunic and neatly curled hair and beard, Assurbanipal pursues his quarry.*

# A MONARCH'S MIGHTY DEEDS

Lured by dreams of conquest and the promise of spoils, Assyria's warrior-kings built one of the mightiest nations of antiquity. By the Seventh Century B.C., King Assurbanipal reigned over an empire that extended from Egypt to Iran. Like most Assyrian rulers, he was a man of action; he led his own troops into battle, and in times of peace displayed his valor hunting lions. Assurbanipal was also a priest and scholar. He built temples, assembled an immense library and, with the aid of scribes, composed scores of citations to himself. These, together with powerfully wrought bas-relief sculptures unearthed from his ruined palace at Nineveh, offer a ringing—and self-satisfied—chronicle of his exploits.

I AM ASSURBANIPAL, KING OF THE UNIVERSE, KING OF ASSYRIA, FOR WHOM ASSUR,
KING OF THE GODS, AND ISHTAR, LADY OF BATTLE, HAVE DECREED
A DESTINY OF HEROISM. . . . THE GOD NERGAL CAUSED ME TO UNDERTAKE EVERY FORM OF
HUNTING ON THE PLAIN, AND ACCORDING TO MY PLEASURE . . . I WENT FORTH. . . .
ON THE PLAIN SAVAGE LIONS, FIERCE CREATURES OF THE MOUNTAINS, ROSE AGAINST ME.

In one of the Nineveh reliefs, spec-
tators clamber excitedly up a wood-
ed hillside that overlooked the royal
hunting ground. Though the King often pursued wild animals in the plains
near the city, the game for this day's
sport was probably specially stocked.
Later, caged lions would be turned
loose into an enclosed field, where
the King would battle them with arrows or spears. At the top of the
hill is a solid, archlike monument
that bears a bas-relief of Assurbanipal slaying a lion from his chariot.

Picking out his weapons, Assurbanipal tests a bow from the selection piled at his feet by a kneeling servant. Retainers standing behind him hold spare arrows, lances and a shield. In addition to all these, the King carries a dagger and a long iron sword, suspended in a sheath from his left hip.

Eager for the chase, a giant mastiff strains at his leash, held by an armed retainer. Like the other hunting reliefs from Assurbanipal's palace, this one shows the powerful forms, feeling for naturalistic detail and the precise execution that characterize the greatest masterpieces of Assyrian art.

The young of the lions thrived in countless numbers. . . . They grew
ferocious through their devouring of herds, flocks and people . . .

In my sport I seized . . . a fierce lion of the plain by his ears.
With the aid of Assur and Ishtar . . . I pierced his body with my lance.

In the forefront of the action, Assurbanipal plunges his spear
down the gullet of a charging lion. Riding bareback—the Assyrians used cloth blankets instead of saddles—he leads a spare horse
that he will use if his original mount is mauled. Since the dawn
of history, lions had been a constant menace in the marshes of
Mesopotamia. One Assyrian monarch, who ruled some four centuries before Assurbanipal, claimed that he killed 1,000 of them.

Upon the lions which I slew, I rested
the fierce bow of the goddess Ishtar.
I offered a sacrifice over them
and poured on them a libation of wine.

The great gods, in their council . . .
caused me to attain unto the priesthood,
which I desired. The offerings I brought
were pleasing unto them. The sanctuaries of
the great gods, my lords, I restored.

The hunt over and the last lion dispatched by arrows (left), King Assurbanipal, seen below, has put on his ceremonial robe and headdress in order to give thanks to the gods. In his role as priest, he is shown pouring wine over four dead lions, while two servants (far left) bring in the body of a fifth.

Other attendants hold the King's weapons and his horse, fan him with fly whisks and strum sacred music on a harp. Incense burns on a tall column next to an altar bearing sacrifices. The rituals accompanying the hunt suggest that it had a religious significance, with the King, representing strength and virtue, vanquishing the forces of destruction.

FROM MY CHILDHOOD, THE GREAT GODS WHO DWELL IN HEAVEN AND ON EARTH HAVE GRANTED ME THEIR FAVOR. LIKE REAL FATHERS THEY RAISED ME, AND INSTRUCTED ME IN THEIR EXALTED WAYS. THEY TAUGHT ME TO WAGE BATTLE AND COMBAT, TO GIVE THE SIGNAL FOR THE SKIRMISH AND TO DRAW UP THE LINE OF BATTLE. . . . THEY MADE MY ARMS POWERFUL AGAINST MY FOES, WHO FROM MY YOUTH TO MY MANHOOD WERE AT ENMITY WITH ME.

For the armies of huntsmen who attended Assurbanipal, the baiting of lions was a prelude to a far more rigorous type of conflict—battle against men; the lessons of discipline and valor learned during the hunt were indispensable training for war.

Armed retainers like those shown here, who ringed the hunting field to prevent the lions from escaping, formed the nucleus of Assyria's crack infantry troops. Additional drilling in the weapons and tactics of the day—the Assyrians were among the first to deploy their infantry in formal lines of battle—helped to transform them into one of the most powerful fighting forces of early times.

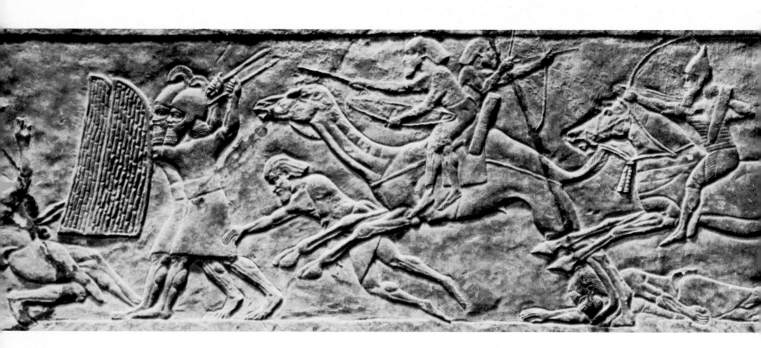

One of Assyria's major conflicts grew out of a family feud between Assurbanipal and his brother, Shamashshumukin, who ruled neighboring Babylon. Though Shamashshumukin was nominally Assurbanipal's vassal, he formed a subversive alliance with the Arabians of the desert and with the Elamite nation in Iran. In 651 B.C. he revolted. Infuriated, Assurbanipal stormed and destroyed Babylon, and then turned to subdue his brother's allies. In these bas-reliefs his armies are seen routing the Arabians, whose scantily clad soldiers, though mounted on camels (right), were no match for the heavily armored Assyrians on foot and horse.

In my ninth campaign I mustered my armies; against Uaite, King of Arabia, I took the straight road. Violating the oath sworn to me and not remembering the good I had done him, he had cast off the yoke of my sovereignty. . . .

I slew great numbers of his warriors, an immeasurable defeat I inflicted upon him. All the people of Arabia who had risen up with him I cut down with the sword.

LIKE THE ONSET OF A TERRIBLE
HURRICANE I OVERWHELMED
ELAM IN ITS ENTIRETY, I CUT OFF
THE HEAD OF TEUMMAN, THEIR
BRAGGART KING, WHO HAD
PLOTTED EVIL. IN COUNTLESS
NUMBERS I KILLED HIS WARRIORS,
AND ALIVE WITH MY HANDS I
SEIZED HIS FIGHTERS. . . .

HAMANU, ELAM'S ROYAL CITY,
I BESIEGED, I CAPTURED . . .
I DESTROYED IT, I DEVASTATED
IT, I BURNED IT WITH FIRE.

Assurbanipal's greatest successes were against
the Elamites, whose cities were no match against
his elaborate siege tactics. In this scene three
attackers scale fortifications with a ladder, while
others, protecting themselves with their shields,
try to breach the city's mud-brick walls with
iron picks. Though apparently outnumbered
three to one, the Assyrians remain unscathed;
wounded Elamites, however, tumble like dates
from a palm tree to drown in the river below.

I am Assurbanipal, the great King, the mighty King,
King of the Universe, King of Assyria, King of the world's four regions,
King of Kings, unrivaled Prince, who at the command of Assur . . .
holds sway from the Upper to the Lower Sea,
and has brought into submission at his feet all princes.

Celebrating his victories, Assurbanipal reclines on a couch in the garden of his palace at Nineveh and drinks a bowl of wine with his queen, Assursharrat, seated at his feet. Servants fan the royal couple with fly whisks and offer trays of delicacies. At the left, next to a musician plucking the strings of a harp, a grim battle trophy hangs from the branches of a stylized tree—the head of the traitorous Teumman, the vanquished King of the Elamites.

# 4

# THE BUSTLING PEOPLE

"Look at it still today: the outer wall where the cornice runs, it shines with the brilliance of copper; and the inner wall, it has no equal. . . . Climb upon the wall of Uruk [Erech]; walk along it, I say; regard the foundation terrace and examine the building; is it not burnt brick and good?"

These lines inviting admiration of the walls of Erech are from the epic tale about Gilgamesh, the king who led Erech to hegemony over all Sumer around the 27th Century B.C. Their words eloquently express the patriotic pride with which the ancient Mesopotamian viewed his native city.

Some of these cities were indeed magnificent, with great public buildings, landscaped parks, and streets arranged in a grid pattern. For example, Agade, built by Sargon the Great in the 24th Century B.C., and whose site has yet to be discovered, was reputed to have been a splendid city; according to one contemporary inscription, "the dwellings of Agade were filled with gold, its bright-shining houses were filled with silver. . . . Its walls reached skyward like a mountain. . . ." Also imposing were such carefully laid out Assyrian capitals as Calah and Dur-Sharrukin. And the Babylon rebuilt by Nebuchadrezzar II aroused the wonder of the entire ancient world.

These great metropolises, however, were exceptional. Most Mesopotamian cities were expansions of the region's prehistoric villages and towns and therefore lacked the benefit of urban planning. But while the physical image of the Mesopotamian city underwent changes and improvements over the centuries, many of its less tangible aspects were impervious to time; social, political, religious and economic patterns that arose in the world's first urban communities, those of the Sumerians, largely characterized all later Mesopotamian cities.

Behind the defense walls that encircled a typical Mesopotamian city, most of the streets were narrow, winding lanes, unpaved and untended. Nor was there any municipal sewage or garbage disposal system; all refuse was flung lustily from the close-packed, mud-brick houses into the street, where it accumulated until it rose above the level of the thresholds. Here and there the larger dwelling of some well-to-do man stood out from its neighbors, but the average house was no more

STYLIZED PORTRAITS, *these statuettes of bearded men, a shaven priest, and a woman clad in a tunic reflect the features and costumes of Mesopotamian townspeople. Their eyes are wide in the tradition of Mesopotamian votive figurines, and their hands clasp libation cups used in religious ceremonies.*

than a thick-walled compound consisting of several windowless rooms with shoulder-high doors arranged around an open court. Large sections of the city, therefore, were drab and unimpressive.

It is people who make a city, however, more than houses and streets, and the Mesopotamians found their urban life exciting, exhilarating and, at times, inspiring.

In every city there were a few broad streets where the citizen and his family could take a leisurely stroll, meet and greet their friends and acquaintances, observe and comment on the passing scene and in general find close communion with their fellow men. Then there was the busy bazaar, and, according to Sir Leonard Woolley, who excavated such an area at Ur, it probably differed but little from the bazaars found in Near Eastern towns today—a maze of narrow passages shielded from the blazing sun by awnings and lined with booths. Here the city dweller could choose his daily groceries from a wide variety of foodstuffs that included onions, beans and cucumbers, dates and apples and other fruits, cheese and spices, dried fish, mutton, pork, duck. Here, too, he could find displayed alongside the pots, clothing, and other local products such imported luxuries as ivory combs from India or carnelian beads from Iran. Woolley's findings at Ur also indicate that there may have been restaurants in the vicinity of the bazaar where shoppers could pause for a dish of fried fish or grilled meat.

Each city also had its beckoning public square set amid the haphazard blocks of houses. Here there were many entertainments and amusements—wrestling matches, games of chance, recitations by professional storytellers and the like—to tempt the schoolboy to loiter on his way to classes. As for the restless, pleasure-bent older citizen, there was the roistering tavern where he could enjoy the ancient version of "wine, women and song."

Supplying spiritual comfort and consolation were the lofty temple and its still loftier, shrine-crowned ziggurat reaching toward the sky. Here images of the great gods were sheltered, clothed and offered food by learned priests familiar with the needs and demands of the heavenly hosts.

According to the belief shared by Sumerian, Babylonian and Assyrian alike, the well-being of his community depended entirely upon the favor of the gods. Most important was the good will of the city's protective or patron deity, who in theory —although not in practice—owned not only the city itself and all its inhabitants but also its farms, orchards and outlying towns.

Entrusted with the rule of this celestially owned property was a mortal, a king presumably approved by the god to serve as his earthly representative. In the earliest Sumerian cities the king was elected by a bicameral assembly of the free citizens—an upper house of elders and a lower house of men of arms-bearing age. He held office only for the duration of an emergency, usually a war, and he was dependent upon the assembly's consent in all matters of major importance. But after about 2800 B.C. kingship became more permanent and eventually it became hereditary. Nevertheless, the democratic feature of council consultation and approval established in early Sumer persisted, and influenced the rule of all later Mesopotamian monarchs.

In administering the god's estate the king had many obligations, secular and religious, which he executed with the assistance of a vast bureaucracy of advisers, overseers, inspectors, scribes and other officials. First and foremost it was the ruler's duty to defend his city and its lands from enemy attacks and to extend its territory, domination and influence. This meant, of course, warfare and all that goes with it: the upkeep of the city's walls, the raising and organizing of armies, leadership in battle and skill in the use of diplomatic ploys.

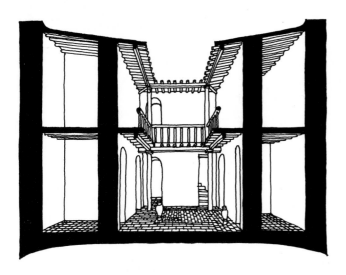

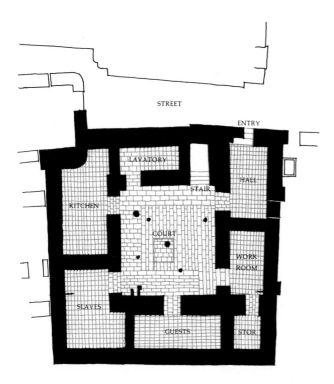

MESOPOTAMIAN DWELLINGS, *like the 4,000-year-old town house at Ur shown in section above, faced inward to an open court, much like Middle Eastern houses today. Steps led down from the street to the ground floor, which was devoted to various domestic functions and a reception room for guests (one possible arrangement is shown in the plan below). A staircase led to the galleried second floor, where the family lived under a sloping roof of timbers, thatch and mud.*

Other duties charged to the king were more constructive and productive. As traditional head of the clergy, one of his most sacred obligations was the building and repairing of his city's temples. As chief overseer of public works, it was up to him to maintain and expand the irrigation canals lacing the city's farmlands and to improve the network of larger navigable canals that carried traffic from the city and its satellite settlements to those of neighboring rulers. Virtually every Mesopotamian monarch who left written records boasted of his temple-building activities and of the new canals that he had dug and the old ones he had ordered repaired or enlarged. Kings also prided themselves on keeping the roads and highways in good traveling condition throughout their territories. For example, Shulgi, one of the kings of Ur in the 21st Century B.C., describes himself as a "nimble, swift traveler over the highways of the land" and exults in having built a series of landscaped roadhouses where travelers might spend a refreshing night.

In the sphere of ethics and morals, it was the ruler's responsibility to promote and preserve law and justice in his realm: to see to it that the poor and the weak were not oppressed, that widows and orphans were not victimized, that the ordinary citizen did not suffer at the hands of overbearing and corrupt officials. To make people aware of their legal rights and thus help to prevent the miscarriage of justice, kings promulgated regulations, edicts and law codes.

The Mesopotamians' passion for law and justice, however, did not have its origins solely in lofty ideals. It stemmed also from a competitive and individualistic temperament, and a high regard for private property. As early as 2500 B.C., soon after writing had been invented, some Mesopotamians had begun to inscribe their transactions—actual contracts and deeds of sale for houses, fields and even slaves—on tablets of clay. These documents

spelled out, in permanent form that could easily be referred to at any time, agreements for dealings between people. Since they established precedents for future actions, they led inevitably to one of the Mesopotamians' greatest contributions to civilization, a logical system of written law.

The earliest known written code of laws and the prototype of all later ones—Sumerian, Babylonian and Assyrian—is that of Ur-Nammu, who reigned over the Sumerian city of Ur about 2100 B.C. Better preserved and more comprehensive, however, is the law code drawn up by Hammurabi of Babylon. Although it dates from about three centuries after Ur-Nammu's, its nearly 300 tersely written laws indirectly provide a revealing portrait of ancient Mesopotamian society and a way of life that saw little substantial change in the course of two or three thousand years.

Hammurabi's code is primarily a collection of case-law describing all sorts of crimes and misdemeanors and specifying the diverse and dire punishments to be meted out for them. Mesopotamian society apparently had its share of murderers, thieves and grafters as well as its adulterers and corner-cutting housebuilders. One law, for example, states that "if the wife of a man has been caught while lying with another man, they shall bind them and throw them into the water. If the husband of the woman wishes to spare his wife, then the king in turn may spare his subject." Another law provides

that "if a builder constructed a house for a man, but did not make his work strong, with the result that the house which he built collapsed and so has caused the death of the owner of the house, that builder shall be put to death."

But, despite its seamier revelations, Hammurabi's law code, like its Sumerian predecessors and the Assyrian codes that succeeded it, in general portrays a stable and well-organized society in which law and order played a predominant role, and one in which even the lowliest individual person was not without some legal protection.

The fabric of that society was composed of three distinct classes: an aristocracy, a majority of common citizens and a minority of slaves. Comprising the aristocracy were a number of rich and powerful families from which came the temple's more important priests and from which the ruler drew his counselors, ambassadors, generals and other high-ranking officials. The wealth and influence of these aristocratic families stemmed primarily from their large landholdings, some of which embraced hundreds of arable acres. For while the god—and thus his home, the temple—was presumed to be sole proprietor of the city's land, actually only a portion of that land was reserved by the temple for the maintenance of its personnel. The rest belonged to the palace or individual citizens, and it was through purchase from less affluent citizens that the great landowners acquired much of their estates.

WOMEN'S HEADDRESSES, *as indicated by these Sumerian statuettes, reveal a startling variety. The two views of the head at far left show a pleated linen turban that concealed all the hair except a thin band framing the face. The style shown next to this permitted women to let their hair flow loosely down the back, with only a ribbon circling the head. The third woman's hair is crowned by a tall headdress, which in turn is covered with a shawl; the last wears a massive helmet and curls that cluster on her shoulders.*

At the opposite extreme of the social scale were the slaves. In the cities of Sumer most of these were the property of the temple, the palace or the wealthy estates. However, by Babylonian and Assyrian times it was not uncommon to find several slaves included in the average household. Nor did slaves consist entirely of prisoners of war; pressed by debt or hunger, a free citizen might sell his children or even himself and his entire family into slavery. But the life of a well-behaved slave in Mesopotamia was not one of unremitting hardship: he was legally entitled to take part in business, to borrow money and to purchase his freedom.

Between the two social extremes—the aristocratic estate owners and the slaves—were the commoners who comprised the bulk and backbone of society. These were the city's productive workers—the architects, scribes and merchants, farmers, cattle breeders and fishermen, the smiths, carpenters, leatherworkers, potters and brickmakers. Many of these possessors of specialized skills or occupations were employed by the wealthiest "landlord" in town, the temple, and in return for their services either were allotted small plots of cultivable land or received rations of wool for clothing, and of food. According to the records of one Sumerian temple, the establishment counted among its workers 100 fishermen, 90 herdsmen, 125 sailors, pilots and oarsmen, 25 scribes and 20 to 25 craftsmen of various categories. Many other specialized workers

were dependents of the palace or labored on the estates of the aristocracy and were probably paid in much the same manner as the temple employees. In addition, there were craftsmen who engaged in free enterprise, selling their wares in the bazaar for payment in kind or in a standard weight of silver.

While the prosperity of a Mesopotamian city depended upon the combined efforts and skills of all its productive workers, two occupations were especially vital to the maintenance of urban life. One was that of the farmer, who raised the cereals that provided the staple food for king, free citizen and slave alike. The other was that of the traveling merchant and trader, who ranged near and far, exchanging the city's surplus goods for commodities that could not be obtained locally.

Since prehistoric times, when Mesopotamia was dotted with small agricultural towns and villages, the farmer had been the mainstay of the region's economy. But with the rise of populous cities in Sumer, Babylonia and Assyria—some with over a hundred thousand mouths to feed—the role of the farmer became more important than ever.

Wheat was grown on the farmlands surrounding a city, but the grain most extensively cultivated was barley, which grew more readily in Mesopotamia's rather alkaline and saline soil. Its kernels could be beaten into coarse particles and cooked as a kind of porridge, or they could be ground into flour and baked into the flat, unleavened bread

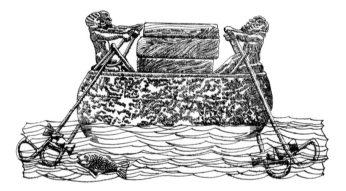

that is still eaten all over the Near East. Barley, too, was the basis for the protein-rich beer that the ancient Mesopotamian enjoyed.

By the Third Millennium B.C., or perhaps even earlier, the Mesopotamian farmer had learned to follow an annual agricultural timetable that produced a bountiful yield. One of the most remarkable documents that has come down to us is a farmer's almanac of the 18th Century B.C., containing explicit guidance to ensure a successful crop. The almanac begins with instructions for the inundation of the farmer's field, probably in May or June, preparatory to plowing, and describes each important step to be taken until the grain is harvested, winnowed and cleaned. In moistening the field for plowing, for example, the farmer is told to ". . . keep a sharp eye on the openings of the dikes, ditches and mounds [so that] when you flood the field the water will not rise too high in it. . . . Let shod oxen trample it for you; after having its weeds ripped out [by them and] the field made level ground, dress it evenly with narrow axes weighing [no more than] two thirds of a pound each." The correct seeding procedure is also described in detail, and the farmer is cautioned to ". . . keep your eye on the man who puts in the barley seed. Let him drop the grain uniformly two fingers deep. . . . If the barley seed does not sink in

properly, change your share, the 'tongue of the plow.'" Finally, the farmer is warned not to "let the barley bend over on itself" but to "harvest it at the moment [of its full] strength."

If the farmer's sphere of activity was limited to his fields and the granaries of his city, that of the traveling merchant and trader was virtually boundless. It was he who kept the cities of Mesopotamia in contact not only with one another but with many distant parts of the ancient world as well. It was he, too, who created the bazaar that added immensely to the pleasures of city life.

Even the region's early villages probably had their small-time tradesmen who bartered the products of one settlement for those of a neighbor's. Long-distance foreign trade, however, was essential to the Mesopotamian cities. For while they produced grain in surplus and their herds of sheep provided an overabundance of wool, they had insufficient timber, stone or metal for building or for the luxuries craved by the temples, palaces, wealthy estates and by their citizens at large.

So came into being the venturesome merchant-entrepreneurs. Over the centuries these risk-taking, keen-minded traders learned to lead their donkey caravans across the desolate Syrian Desert to the Mediterranean coast, through the passes of the Zagros ranges into Iran and as far north as Lake Van in Armenia. They plied the Persian Gulf in boats, reaching far-off India, and crossed the Arabian Sea to trade with Somaliland and Ethiopia in Africa. In exchange for the grain, wool and textiles that made up their load or cargo they brought back gold, silver, copper and lead, such badly needed timber as cedar and cypress, and luxury items that included ivory, pearls and shells, as well as malachite, carnelian, lapis lazuli and other semiprecious stones. Together with these exotic wares the merchants brought back beguiling tales of foreign peoples with strange languages, unusual customs and mysterious beliefs and rites. In fact, it was the traveling merchants even more than the learned priests and scribes who expanded the horizon of their fellow citizens and helped to make the Mesopotamian city an exhilarating and sophisticated metropolis.

Augmenting this broad picture of Mesopotamian urban life are numerous details gleaned from excavated tablets with cuneiform inscriptions, the evidence of building ruins and scraps of everyday objects. Excavations have shown, for instance, that while an ordinary member of the working class dwelt in a humble, single-story house of mud-brick, a farmer, merchant, scribe or artisan whose services had earned him prosperity above the average lived in comfortable circumstances. Remains of homes of fairly well-to-do Sumerian citizens found at Ur and dating from around the 20th Century B.C. reflect a surprisingly high standard of living, and they differ only in minor details from most of their later Assyrian and Babylonian counterparts.

Such a house in its day was a two-story structure made of the kiln-baked and sun-dried brick, neatly whitewashed inside and out and well-insulated against the blazing Mesopotamian sun by walls that were sometimes as much as six feet thick. From a small entrance vestibule one stepped down into a brick-paved court provided with a central drain to carry off water during the winter rainy season. Opening off the court were the doors to the ground-floor rooms. The number of these rooms might vary from house to house, but typically they consisted of a chamber where guests were received and entertained, and where they might spend the night; a lavatory; the kitchen with its fireplaces and utensils of clay, stone and copper; a servants' room and a general workroom that probably also served as a storeroom. There may also have been on the ground floor a small chapel where the household gods were worshiped, and below some houses were mausoleums for the burial of the family dead.

A flight of stairs led up to the second story, where a wooden gallery about three feet wide, and supported by wooden poles, ran around the courtyard, leading to the family's private living quarters. A ladder probably gave access to the flat or slightly sloping roof, on which the family often slept on clear summer nights. The house was simply but comfortably furnished with beds and couches, chairs and tables, and there were wood or wicker-work chests for storing clothes. Rugs covered the floors and colored hangings decorated the walls.

As might be expected, kings lived on a vastly more lavish scale, and evidence of this comes from Mari, the city in western Mesopotamia destroyed by Hammurabi in the 18th Century B.C. Mari's palace, a gigantic complex covering almost seven acres and consisting of open courtyards and nearly 300 rooms—some of them beautifully decorated with wall paintings—is remarkably well preserved and is considered an outstanding example of the abode and administrative headquarters of a Mesopotamian ruler. The thousands of cuneiform documents making up its archives, combined with the architectural remains, enable scholars to reconstruct many details of palace life and to provide a picture of court routine that saw little variation down through the centuries.

The ancient Mesopotamians began their day soon after sunrise in order to take advantage of the relatively cool morning hours, and morning seems to have been the time that the king of Mari chose to hold his public audience.

Enthroned on a raised platform and surrounded by his ministers and members of his guard, the ruler solemnly received ambassadors from other courts. In addition to their diplomatic messages concerning commercial alliances, requests for military aid and the like, these emissaries frequently brought presents from their monarchs; the Mari archives reveal that a king in northern Syria once sent the king of Mari a gift of fine wine and promised more. "If there is no good wine . . . for you to drink," he wrote, "send me a message and I will send you good wine."

Much of the king's daily audience was naturally given over to affairs pertaining to his own realm. Reports from officials administering the kingdom's various towns had to be heard and appropriate advice or instructions had to be issued; lawsuits too serious to be handled by any lesser authority were brought to the ruler's attention and his decision

sought; if drought had struck some pastoral district, it was up to the king to arrange for the flocks to graze elsewhere; if a nomadic tribe had invaded a cultivated area, the king had to dispatch troops to prevent further incursions. Even a matter as trivial as the runaway wife of a private citizen was not beneath the king's notice, and his aid was solicited in bringing about her return.

Since the king was the earthly representative of the city's patron god, various religious activities played a prominent part in the royal routine. These might include visiting the god's temple to report to that deity on the welfare of the land, offering sacrifices to ensure the god's continuing protection, or officiating at rituals, such as the purification of the site for a new temple.

Not all of the king's day was occupied with the serious business of ruling, however. It is known, for example, that one of the daily meals at the palace of Mari was a royal banquet attended by distinguished visitors and by those nobles to whom the ruler wished to show special honor. There were also court entertainments featuring music, dancing and recitals. Female slaves were specially trained in the use of such instruments as harps, lyres and reed pipes, and poets and minstrels amused the king with performances of their works.

From the brilliance of their royal courts to the well-regulated life of the rest of their society, the cities that evolved and developed in the Land Between the Rivers were indeed an outstanding contribution to human progress. Without the order and security provided within their walls there could have been no flowering of the complex elements that make up a civilization—writing, a legal system, a high level of political organization, specialization of arts and crafts.

The weaving together of these elements, first accomplished in ancient Mesopotamia, produced the pattern of urban existence that survives to this day.

DAWN ON A MARSH LAGOON *finds a tribesman paddling his slim canoe, as did his early forebears, across a desolate expanse of water and reeds.*

# A TIMELESS LIFE IN THE MARSHES

Since the first glimmer of civilization, life has scarcely changed for the people who live in the broad marshlands of southern Mesopotamia, where the Tigris and Euphrates rivers flow together. Here, in a seemingly endless landscape of swamp, canebrakes and shallow lagoons, time passes virtually unnoticed, unmarked by watches or calendars. The memories of the marsh dwellers go back only a few generations; but their lives follow patterns established 60 centuries ago, in the days when the first nomadic tribes settled in this watery land.

Like their distant predecessors, the men of the marshes catch fish in the lagoons, bake unleavened bread in crude ovens, herd water buffalo, and build arched huts of towering reeds. There are a few differences, of course. Today's marsh dwellers, who claim Arab descent, worship Allah rather than the gods of ancient Sumer, and they import textiles and a few firearms for hunting from the outside world. But the round of their daily lives is an echo of an age when arts were rudimentary, history unwritten and cities not yet known.

*Photographs by Tor Eigeland*

A MORNING'S ACTIVITIES *begin as two men embark from their village (background) to gather reeds, while a pair of water buffalo wallow nearby.*

# A WORLD ON WATER

The world began, according to a Babylonian myth, when the god Marduk built a platform of reeds and earth on the face of a primordial universe where "all the lands were sea." In much the same way, the marsh tribes of today erect villages on artificial islands built up of reeds and mud. Each house stands on its own island, which also doubles as a barnyard for the family's water buffalo. These animals, first domesticated by the Sumerians around 4000 B.C., are essential to the marsh economy, providing milk for food, as well as dung, which is burned for fuel.

A HERD OF BUFFALO, *grouped around a barn built of marsh reeds, is seen in a clay impression made from an ancient Sumerian identification seal.*

AN ANCIENT FACADE, *depicted in a Sumerian carving, shows the arched roof and plumelike column tops of a typical reed house.*

# A LASTING LEGACY OF REED ARCHITECTURE

In a land barren of trees and without stone quarries, the marsh tribes build their houses of the only material available, the fragile marsh reeds. The resulting buildings—tunnel-like structures with curving roofs—are survivals of one of the oldest architectural styles in history: the reed huts of the ancient Mesopotamians *(above)*.

These early builders employed the first known columns, arches and vaulted roofs. Today's marsh dwellers use the same elements in virtually the same way. They build a framework by setting two rows of bundled reeds into the ground to make columns, then bending and tying their tops together to form arches *(left)*. Crosspieces are added, and the structure is roofed over with reed matting.

A MODERN FRAMEWORK *of arched columns and rafters is erected by two tribesmen. Since the columns, crosspieces and mats are prefabricated, an entire house can be built in a few hours.*

# THE DAILY TASKS
# OF SURVIVAL

In the bleak environment of the marshes
—where winter gales hamper transportation and spring floods sometimes wash out
whole villages—mere survival is a dawn-
to-dusk battle. The tasks that sustain life
in these villages are themselves survivals
from the distant past.

Rice, introduced about 1000 B.C., is the
staple food. It is planted sprout by sprout
in shallow paddies, harvested by hand,
and carried in flat-bottomed canoes to the
villages. Sometimes the floods, which help
irrigate the dry croplands outside the
marshes, completely swamp the paddies in
the interior and destroy a season's crop.

The only transportation on the marshes
is by canoe. Wood for building these vessels must be imported from northern Iraq,
along with bitumen, an asphaltlike substance used for waterproofing the plank-
ing of the hulls. Every year, the old bitumen is scraped off and a new coat applied
to keep the boats seaworthy. In exchange
for timber and bitumen, the marsh dwellers barter mats woven from marsh reeds.

WINNOWING RICE, *two women pour threshed
grain from baskets in front of a reed hut. The
chaff blows away as the kernels fall into a pile.*

WATERPROOFING CANOES, *one worker (left) spreads a coat of fresh bitumen on a hull, while a second man makes repairs on another boat.*

GRINDING FLOUR, *women pound rice kernels in a stone mortar. The rice flour will be baked into coarse bread in earthenware ovens.*

POLING A REED CANOE, *which has a high, curving prow and stern, a Sumerian boatman ferries a passenger in this impression of a 5,000-year-old seal.*

FISHING WITH SPEARS, *marsh dwellers stand in their gracefully curved canoes and plunge metal-tipped shafts into the reed beds at the edge of a lagoon.*

# AN AGE-OLD REFUGE AMONG THE REEDS

Despite their hardships, the marshes have been a perennial refuge for hunters and fishermen. Duck and heron breed by the thousands in the canebrakes, where for centuries men have snared them for food. Carp and eel, speared or netted in the lagoons, fed the early Mesopotamians; today, the marsh dwellers go after the same fish with long bamboo poles fitted with five-pronged metal tips *(below).*

In the past, the marshes also provided another type of refuge—for men escaping justice. In some parts of ancient Mesopotamia, the word for fisherman became synonymous with "outlaw." During the Assyrian empire, a rebellion against authority by marsh tribes became so widespread that the king, Sennacherib, mounted a punitive expedition, embarking his troops in local canoes. At that time, the boats were fashioned of reeds coated with pitch; but to help ease them through the canebrakes, they were built with the same shallow draft and crescent-shaped prows *(left)* as today's wooden craft.

AT THE END OF DAY, *the setting sun outlines symbols of the marsh dwellers' livelihood: bundles of cut reeds, the tall prow of a canoe, a bull calf. Plan*

by the government of Iraq to drain the marshes for use as farmlands may eventually mean the passing of this way of life, as old as civilization itself.

# 5

# FAITH, MYTHS
# AND RITES

The religion of ancient Mesopotamia is the oldest of which we have written records. Based on Sumerian beliefs, it provided spiritual and ethical guidance for the affairs of men, offered an acceptable explanation for the ultimate mysteries of life and death, and bequeathed a heritage of colorful mythology that strongly influenced later religions.

The Babylonians and Assyrians, who in their turn succeeded the Sumerians, took over most of the Sumerian gods and religious practices. This is not to say that the later priests and poets followed slavishly their Sumerian prototypes. But, for the most part, they were unable to escape the all-pervading influence of their Sumerian inheritance.

This complex body of law and story forthrightly confronted the fundamental questions that have always troubled mankind: Who are we? Where are we? How did we get here? The Mesopotamian answers were direct and meaningful, although quite wrong in the light of modern science. The earth, which they believed to be a flat disk, was surrounded by a vast hollow space enclosed in the over-arching heaven—together forming a universe called *An-ki*, "heaven-earth." The space above the earth and below heaven was filled with a material to which they gave the name *lil*. All around heaven and earth—top, bottom and sides—rolled the sea, infinite and restless, miraculously anchoring the universe. The omnipresence of the waters convinced the Mesopotamians that they were primeval and eternal—the source of all things. From the waters had come the universe, that is, the heavenly arch and the disk of earth. The airy expanding atmosphere in between, separating "Father Heaven" from "Mother Earth," also produced the shining stars, the sun and the moon, thus setting the stage for the creation of man and the establishment of civilization.

It was natural for the ancient thinkers and sages to conceive of the creation of the universe and its organization in human terms. All human society as they knew it, all human activity, was directed by people. The universe, too, they imagined, must therefore be run by anthropomorphic, or human-like beings, generally unperceivable to lowly mortals. The mighty beings in charge of the universe must be more powerful and effective than their

A GOLDEN GOAT, *found in a Sumerian grave at Ur, symbolized fertility and may once have supported a tray of incense during religious rites. The animal's head and legs, as well as the flowering tree, were made of wood overlaid with gold; his coat is of shell, his horns and eyes of lapis lazuli.*

THE SUN-GOD UTU, *one of the chief Sumerian deities, lights the world with rays issuing from his shoulders. He was also the god of justice, and carved out judgments with his saw.*

MOTHER EARTH, *Ninhursag was the source of all life. From her came the birth of plants; to emphasize that role she wears a leafy crown and holds a branch denoting fertility.*

human counterparts on earth, and these beings must live forever, for the unthinkable alternative was utter confusion at their death. Unseeable, boundlessly powerful and immortal, they were gods, in Sumerian *dingir*. There had to be many such gods to guide the innumerable physical and spiritual components of the world, and the Mesopotamians had no difficulty in supplying this need by inventing new gods when the occasion arose. The surviving documents show that, even by 2500 B.C., the roll call of Sumerian gods, the pantheon, consisted of hundreds of deities, each with his own name and sphere of activity.

In spite of its size and complexity, the pantheon created by the imaginative sages usually operated smoothly and harmoniously. The gods were ranked hierarchically according to their importance, influence and power. Greatest of all were the gods in control of the four major realms of the universe: An, god of heaven, Enlil, the air-god, Enki, the

water-god, and Ninhursag, the great mother-earth goddess. These four were the supreme deities, who planned and created the components of the universe, and placed them in the charge of one or another of their offspring, the administrative gods. Creation was not too difficult or laborious, for once the gods had decided what they wanted to do, they had merely to voice their plan of action and the thing was done. This idea developed into a credo that was shared as an accepted article of faith throughout the Near East: the Word of God —or of various gods—has the power, of itself, to create something out of nothingness.

Even the most potent and wisest of the deities resembled man in their earthly activities. They feasted, took wives, had children and were—depending on the occasion—good humored, angry, joyous, sad, selfless, jealous, noble, petty, heartless or charitable. In general, they were in favor of honesty and decency, and against lies and evil; but

LORD OF WATER AND WISDOM, *Enki emits streams from his shoulders. He was the god who gave rulers their intelligence and who provided craftsmen with their skills.*

GODDESS OF LOVE AND WAR, *Inanna stands beside her insignia, gateposts hung with streamers. She was present whenever life was conceived through love or ended in battle.*

to judge from the myths told about them they were far from immaculately sinless.

The gods could travel about when necessary: the sun-god had a chariot, although he occasionally moved on foot. The storm-god reached his destination on a cloud, while the moon-god had a boat at his disposal. Not that the Mesopotamians worried very much about such realistic details, nor did they feel a pressing need to resolve the paradoxes inherent in their polytheistic faith. It probably never occurred to the ancient Mesopotamians to question the inconsistent nature of their deities, who could become seriously ill, who had to eat, sleep and find dwelling places, who battled, massacred enemies and sometimes even died—only to find a new life in the netherworld.

In very early times, beginning in the Fourth Millennium B.C., when the city of Erech was dominant in the land, the leading Sumerian deity seems to have been the heaven-god An. His pre-eminence

comes somewhat as a surprise: since the sea plays so vital a role in creation myths, Nammu, the goddess of the primeval sea, "the mother who gave birth to heaven and earth," might have been expected to head the list. But the divine hierarchy, like the Mesopotamian political scene after which it was patterned, was male-dominated, and An was therefore the reigning monarch. With the decline of Erech, however, An must have lost much of his prestige and ceased to play any significant role in myth or hymn. Most of his powers and prerogatives were conferred upon the air-god Enlil, the guardian deity of the city of Nippur, which became the political and religious center of southern Mesopotamia.

For about a thousand years after 2500 B.C., Enlil continued as supreme ruler of the Sumerian pantheon, and, to some extent, of the Babylonian and Assyrian as well. Enlil is a Sumerian compound word meaning "Lord Air"—he was the moving force in effecting the separation of Father Heaven from Mother Earth, who not long after bore Enlil's offspring. He is therefore described as the "father of the gods," "the king of the universe," "the king of all the lands." Enlil raised up the "seed of the land" from earth, brought into existence "whatever was needful," invented the pickax and gave it to man to advance his agricultural pursuits and thereby bring him prosperity and affluence. The gods were eager for Enlil's blessing. According to one myth, the powerful water-god, Enki of Eridu, after building his resplendent Sea House, journeyed to Enlil's temple, Ekur, in Nippur to obtain his benediction. Another myth tells of the moon-god Nanna, the tutelary deity of far-famed Ur, who wanted to make sure of the well-being of his city. He journeyed to Nippur in a boat loaded with gifts, and offered them for Enlil's generous blessing. No wonder the poets glorified Enlil in such lines as:

Enlil, whose command is far-reaching,
    lofty his word and holy,
Whose pronouncement is unchangeable,
    who decrees destinies unto the distant future,
Whose lifted eye scans the lands,
Whose lifted beam searches the heart of the land,
When father Enlil seats himself broadly on the holy dais,
    the lofty dais,
When he perfects lordship and princeship,
The earth-gods bow down before him,
The heaven-gods humble themselves before him. . . .

It is Enlil who is given credit for the *me* (pronounced "may"), which were a set of "universal laws" governing all existence. The creation of these broad concepts is a remarkable tribute to the originality of the people of Mesopotamia, for they were the first to conceive so speculative a concept.

For the Mesopotamians, the *me* were a response to their yearning for reassurance in a troubling world. They needed to believe that the universe and all its parts, once created, would continue to operate in an orderly and effective manner, not subject to disintegration or deterioration. The *me* devised by Enlil governed everyone and everything in the universe; and mortal men could take comfort in the knowledge that the blue sky, the teeming earth, the dark netherworld, the wild sea, were all acting in accordance with the rules of the gods.

There were more than a hundred *me*, one for each of the aspects of the world and its civilization. There were special *me* for deities and men, lands and cities, palaces and temples, love and law, truth and falsehood, war and peace, music and art, cult and ritual, as well as for all the crafts and professions. Enlil granted these *me* to guide the gods, spelling out their rights, duties, and privileges, bounds and controls, authority and restraint.

*Me* figure prominently in some of the principal Mesopotamian myths about gods. Nonetheless, the elaborate stories played a very small part—if any —in the religious observances. In all except a few instances, the myths are expressions of literary significance. They were written to give pleasure or inspiration, as well as to explain cosmic events and religious beliefs. They are usually enjoyable tales of the gods in love, at war, at their work of creation.

It was an act that seems to have violated one of the *me* that, according to a myth, led to Enlil's undoing; supremely powerful though he was, he had not reckoned with his own violent sexual appetite.

One day, before the creation of man, when only gods lived in the city of Nippur, Enlil was walking along a canal and spied a young goddess, the beautiful Ninlil, bathing in its waters. He was so filled with desire that he determined to possess her then and there. When Ninlil resisted Enlil's advances, pleading that she was too young, he seized her, took her aboard a boat and raped her. This immoral deed violated the very *me* Enlil had himself set up for the orderly operation of the universe.

Thereupon the gods banished their leader to the netherworld. The unfortunate Ninlil, who was to bear the moon-god, Nanna, as a result of the union, followed Enlil to the world below.

Fortunately for man and civilization, by the time Enlil went to the underworld, the *me* had been entrusted to Enki, the god of water (his mother was the sea-goddess Nammu) and wisdom, who kept them safely in the Abzu, his deep-sea shrine.

It was Enki who carried out the actual details of organizing the universe. He began by assigning various degrees of prosperity to the several lands comprising the ancient world, including Sumer and possibly Egypt. He then supplied the things necessary to make the earth fruitful and provide for man's needs: he poured pure water into the Tigris and Euphrates, sowed the marshes and canebrakes with fish and reeds, caused rain to fall on the earth, heaped up grain in the cultivated fields, built stalls and erected sheepfolds. To make sure that all this highly productive labor was not in vain, he appointed special deities to watch over his innovations and see that they were used properly, presumably in accordance with the divine *me*.

Wise as Enki was, and precious as the *me* entrusted to him were for his city, Eridu, he was unable to hold on to them; in his case it was drink rather than passion that brought about the loss. Enki's downfall came at the hands of his daughter Inanna, prototype of the Greek Aphrodite and the Roman Venus. Inanna—the name means "queen of heaven"—was worshiped throughout Mesopotamia as the goddess of love, procreation and fertility. But she was also the special guardian deity of Erech from very early days, and she was determined to make her city the great cultural center of Sumer, and indeed of the whole civilized world. This she would be able to do only by getting hold of the divine *me*. She decided to obtain them from Enki, regardless of the cost.

Setting out on her "Boat of Heaven," she and her attendant Ninshubur went to Enki's temple, the Abzu, where she was greeted warmly and invited to a lavish banquet of barley cake and date wine. The host, Enki, outdid his guest in enjoying the festivities. Somewhat befuddled by wine, he began giving her the *me*, a few at a time. Only too happy to accept the invaluable gifts—possibly inscribed on tablets or embodied in some distinctive symbolic form—Inanna took them, loaded them on her boat, and left swiftly for Erech before the drunken Enki realized what he had done.

Once he was sober, Enki became aware that the *me* were missing. He listened in shocked dismay as his servant Isimud told him of the gifts he had made to Inanna. Filled with remorse over his betrayal of his trust, Enki vowed to recover the *me*. He ordered Isimud, and an assorted complement of sea monsters, to hasten to each of the seven stopping points situated between Eridu and Erech. Isimud was instructed to seize the boat and its cargo, but to let Inanna return freely to her city. All of the rescue attempts were frustrated, however, by Inanna's brave and dependable counselor, Ninshubur, and Inanna and her boat returned safely to Erech. There her happy people watched as the invaluable *me* were brought ashore to establish Erech as the leading city of Sumer.

Enki also had his troubles with another goddess, Ninhursag, who was perhaps the original "Mother Earth." This time, however, it was not drink but food that got him into difficulties, for he ate certain food, a motif reminiscent of the "Paradise" story in the Book of Genesis. The scene of this myth is Dilmun. In Dilmun, according to the poets, no one was ever ill and no one grew old. But Dilmun lacked fresh water until the sun-god Utu, at Enki's command, caused water to well up, and thereafter all kinds of vegetation flourished.

In this paradise, Ninhursag caused eight special

plants to grow after an extremely complicated set of events requiring the conception of successive generations of goddesses, all sired by Enki. Enki was tempted by the plants, and he ordered his servant Isimud to pluck them and bring them to him. When Ninhursag heard that the plants had been eaten, she was furious and uttered a malediction that promised Enki's death. Then she left the council of the gods.

As a result of this curse, Enki fell ill from a sickness affecting eight of his bodily organs. Death neared, his fellow deities mourned, but not a thing could be done for Enki without Ninhursag's presence. Fortunately there was a clever fox on the scene and he, in some unknown manner, was able to entice Ninhursag to return to the assembly. In a happy ending she saved the life of the dying Enki by creating eight deities who restored each of his ailing organs to health.

One other Sumerian myth has a far more compelling interest for Western man. This is the story of the Great Flood, which found an echo in later Akkadian and, of course, Biblical versions. Although the Sumerian version has been gathered from fragments of but one third of a clay tablet, its story can be reconstructed with the aid of Akkadian versions in the following form:

Sometime after man, plants, and animals had been created, and kingship had been established in five special cities, the gods determined to bring the Flood and destroy mankind. (The passage giving the reason for this melancholy judgment is broken away, but possibly relates to disobedience on the part of man.) But, the tale continues, some of the gods were unhappy with the extreme severity of the decree. One of them, Enki, revealed it to Ziusudra (whose name in Akkadian is Utnapishtim), a mortal being noted for his humble obedience and reverence, and counseled him to build a giant boat to ride out the tempestuous Flood, and

so save his own life and "the seed of mankind." Ziusudra faithfully followed the god's directions, and was delivered from destruction, or as the poet puts it:

> After, for seven days [and] seven nights,
> The flood had swept over the land,
> [And] the huge boat had been tossed about by the
>     windstorms on the great waters,
> Utu [the sun-god] came forth, who sheds light
>     on heaven and earth . . .

Following a break in the text, we find Ziusudra prostrating himself before An and Enlil, two of the leading gods of the pantheon, who are so pleased with his god-fearing humility that they give him "life like a god," and "breath eternal," and carry him to the Paradise-like Dilmun, "the place where the sun rises."

For the Mesopotamians, myths such as these must have furnished much-needed relief from their rather sober and chastened world view of man's destiny, which contrasted sharply with the glorious roles they gave to their gods. Man, they were convinced, was fashioned of clay, or, as some said, of clay and the blood of a slaughtered god, and created for one purpose only: to serve the gods by supplying them with food and shelter, so that they might have a respite from the chores of everyday life. Fatalistic and resigned, the Sumerians believed that man was helpless in the face of inscrutable divine wrath and that man's life was beset with uncertainty and haunted by insecurity. Still, death was nothing to look forward to since when man died his spirit descended to the dark and dreary netherworld.

One slippery and elusive moral problem, which has given so much vexation to Western theologians, never troubled the Sumerian thinkers at all—the rather delicate question of free will. Convinced that they were created to be slaves and

servants of the gods, they meekly and submissively accepted the divine decisions, even the inexplicable and seemingly unjustified ones. Nor did they question the capriciousness and eccentricity of the gods in bringing wickedness and baseness, hardship and calamity into the world, because these were to be expected; there were *me* for such unwelcome human traits as "falsehood," "strife," "fear," "lamentation," "the troubled heart," as well as for the cruel afflictions of "floods" and "destruction of cities." A Sumerian who, like the Biblical Job, was burdened with undeserved troubles was taught not to argue and complain in the face of inscrutable misfortune, but to admit that he was, inevitably, a depraved soul, since, as one sage sadly phrased it: "Never was a sinless child born to his mother."

It was too much to expect the gods, and especially the great gods who counted most, to listen and—perhaps—help ordinary men. Enlil, Enki and their peers were too distant, aloof and inaccessible to pay attention to mere mortals and their troubles. What man needed was help at a lower level of divinity. And so there developed the idea of a personal god, a heavenly guardian who looked after a man and his family. It was to this "father" who begot him, that a man addressed his prayers and his pleas. If any small help were to come, it would be through the intercession of this personal deity.

Even with this aid, men could look forward with certainty only to death and descent to the netherworld. The Mesopotamian picture of their final home was blurred and contradictory.

In general, the netherworld was conceived to be a huge cosmic space below the earth, corresponding roughly to heaven, the huge cosmic space above the earth. The souls of the dead went down to the underworld, probably from their last resting places in the earth, although there may have been entryways leading to it in the more important cities of the land. To reach the netherworld the souls had to ferry across a river. Ruling this gloomy domain from a palace barred by seven gates were Nergal and Ereshkigal, who were attended by a variety of gods, including seven Anunnaki who acted as judges, and "dead" gods of the heavens. In addition, there were troops of "devils" called *galla*, who acted as policemen. The entire company, except the *galla*, had to be supplied with all the trappings of mortal life—food, utensils, clothing and so forth.

Even in death there was a strict order of precedence. The souls of kings and high officials occupied the most desirable places. Any newly arrived distinguished dead had to offer sacrifices to their noble predecessors. Conduct in the netherworld, as elsewhere, followed certain rules, which were enforced by Gilgamesh, the great hero immortalized in myth who became a god after his death. The netherworld was in gloomy darkness during earth's daytime; but when the sun set on earth it moved through the place of the dead, and the moon likewise made this trip at the end of each lunar month.

When the deceased arrived in the netherworld

they were judged by the sun-god Utu, and if he ruled favorably, their souls could presumably look forward to a contented existence. In spite of this gleam of hope, Mesopotamians believed that life in the netherworld was at best a dismal reflection of its earthly counterpart. They had little reason to expect a blissful afterlife, no matter how blameless they may have been.

Because of man's subservient position in relation to the gods, it was vitally important that he honor the gods, on certain important occasions, by participating in religious ceremonies. These rites were performed by priests in the sacred temples.

Over the centuries these temples had grown from small, simple shrines to the vast collections of buildings found in the larger cities of Mesopotamia. Temple compounds of this complexity required a large staff headed by an administrator and a spiritual leader, or high priest; sometimes there was also a high priestess. Next in order of rank came a variety of priests, each with specialized duties. One group, just below the highest ranks, conducted the routine ceremonies; other priests pronounced incantations and interpreted omens; still others soothed the gods with music, or were in charge of the sacrificial rites. In addition, there were numerous secular officials, workers and servants who helped to carry on the temple's agricultural and business affairs.

In the temple of every major city in Mesopotamia, daily sacrifices were made to the gods. Meats and vegetables, libations of water, beer and wine were offered, fragrant spices and perfumed incense were burned. These ceremonies were conducted by priests, and by and large, the ordinary citizen took little, if any, part in them. The lay public may have played a more prominent role in the many recurring festivals and several regular monthly feasts at which the rituals were much more dra-

matic and dignified. The most important of these was the New Year holiday that took place in the spring. This required several days of ceremony, centered on the "Sacred Marriage" on New Year's Day between the king, who took the role of Dumuzi (called Tammuz in the Bible), an early ruler of Erech, and a high priestess who played the part of Inanna. This ritual was a re-enactment of a ceremony that, according to legend, was first performed by Dumuzi when he was married to Inanna, who was Erech's patron deity.

The holy nuptials between the king and the goddess had a twofold purpose: to ensure the fertility of the land and—at least so the king hoped—to ensure his long life as a husband of the goddess. The romance inspired a number of different songs and tales revolving about a central rite and theme: the sacred marriage of this mortal king to the goddess, which begins in a mood of wistful yearning, and ends inevitably in bitter frustration and disaster.

According to Mesopotamian myth, the union of Dumuzi and Inanna ended in grim and bitter tragedy for Dumuzi. Ironically, it was the divine marriage through which he hoped to become immortal that led to his downfall, and it was the very goddess Inanna whose love he had so eagerly sought and won that sent him to perdition. Dumuzi, it seems, had failed to reckon with his divine spouse's ambition and pride. All this was told by the bards in a rather baleful tale whose plot ran as follows:

After her marriage to Dumuzi, Inanna, though already Queen of Heaven, set her heart on becoming the mistress of the netherworld as well. There, however, she was put to death by the jealous Ereshkigal, Queen of the Netherworld. Goddess though she was, Inanna would have remained dead forever had not the kindly Enki intervened and succeeded in having her revived by sprinkling her with the "food of life" and the "water of life." But Inanna's perils were not ended. For, according to the *me* of the netherworld, no one—not even a deity—having once passed its portals could ascend again to the world of the living without supplying another who would substitute for him. The resurrected Inanna, allowed to leave the underworld, was escorted by a group of *galla*, the little devils who inhabit the lower regions; the *galla* had orders to return Inanna to the netherworld unless she found a replacement.

Inanna and her devilish attendants wandered from city to city looking for a deity whom the *galla* could carry off as her substitute. The gods of the first two cities she came to put on sackcloth and prostrated themselves before her. Though the *galla* were eager to seize these frightened creatures, Inanna refused to let them do so. However, when Inanna and her ghostly entourage arrived at her own city, Erech, she found Dumuzi sitting on a high throne in a noble robe, only too happy to be free of his aggressive and domineering spouse to whom he would always have to play second fiddle. Furious at this betrayal, Inanna told the demons to take him away. Dumuzi implored the aid of the sun-god Utu, the just judge, who was Inanna's brother and therefore his brother-in-law. Utu took pity on him, and transformed him into a snake, but to no avail. The *galla* caught up with him, tortured him to death and carried him to the netherworld where he would have remained forever as Inanna's surrogate. However, his loving and self-sacrificing sister, the goddess Geshtinanna, agreed to take his place for half the year.

The annual repetition of the Sacred Marriage ceremony seems to have satisfied some deep need of the Mesopotamians for reassurance about their fate in years to come, much as modern man celebrates his survival of the perils of the year and his reaping of the harvest with feasting and rejoicing at Thanksgiving.

The celebration of the New Year festival in the city of Babylon during the First Millennium B.C. included, in addition to the sacred marriage, several features of an obscure Sumerian festival known as *Akitu*. However, it added a number of symbolic and incantatory rites altogether unknown in the earlier times. One of these was the recitation of the *Enuma-Elish*, the creation epic, which drew upon Sumerian myth for some of its subject matter. In the Babylonian version of the *Enuma-Elish*, the hero is Marduk, national god of Babylon. When the Assyrians took over, they substituted their national god, Assur, in this role.

To be sure, much of what we know about this late Babylonian New Year festival comes from a priestly textbook of the Third Century B.C., and some of the details may not have applied in earlier times. By and large, however, the following account of the New Year rites, rituals and ceremonies may be taken to be reasonably credible.

The Babylonian New Year festival lasted 11 days, beginning with the first day of Nisan, the month of the spring equinox. The better part of the first four days was devoted primarily to prayers by the high priest; to the chanting of the *Enuma-Elish*, the epic glorifying Marduk as the leading god of the pantheon; and to the fashioning of two red-garbed, snake-and-scorpion-holding puppets symbolizing evil forces, which were decapitated and then tossed into a blazing fire on the sixth day.

According to the epic, in the beginning there was only watery chaos: Abzu, the sweet waters, and Tiamat, the sea, combined their forces to create the universe and the gods. But then Abzu plotted against the gods, and all-wise Enki destroyed him. Angry Tiamat continued the war against the gods, none of whom was strong enough to withstand her until Marduk, son of Enki, offered to take the field. Marduk, "superb of stature, with lightning glance and virile garb . . . a leader born," asked in return to be chief of the gods.

Gathering in counsel, the assembled deities accepted Marduk's terms, and granted him such power that his word became law. After fierce fighting, Marduk prevailed over Tiamat, and used half her body to make the sky. Then he set the stars and the moon in place and created man out of the blood of a god who had sided with Tiamat. In tribute to Marduk's prowess, the assembly of gods built a majestic shrine to him, and gave a great feast, at which they proclaimed Marduk's 50 names. Then, pleased with their work, the gods turned the world over to man so that they would be able to take their ease.

The Babylonian New Year festival continued with other rituals on the fifth day following the routine prayers and sacrifices; there was a purification ceremony in the course of which the temple was sprinkled with holy water and sanctified with holy oil. A sheep was then beheaded, and its bleeding body was pressed against the temple walls, probably in order to absorb any remaining impurities. This slaughtered animal was then carried out and hurled into the river as a scapegoat. A golden "sky-canopy" was next erected in preparation for the arrival of Nabu, Marduk's son, from nearby Borsippa.

For the first time during the festival, the king himself now appeared in the Esagila, the huge temple complex, and went through a humiliating ritual calculated to make him realize that he was but a humble servant of the gods, and responsible to them for the welfare of his people. The rite began as the high priest removed the king's royal insignia, such as the scepter and his sword, and placed them before the image of Marduk. The high priest then pulled the king's ears, and forced him to bow before the god and recite a negative confession, stressing the fact that he had not mistreated Babylon and its people in any way.

At this point, the high priest returned the royal insignia to the king and then struck him in the face. If the king's eyes filled with tears, it was a sign that Marduk was pleased with him. In the evening of the same day, the king, none the worse for his mortification and abasement before the god and his priest, participated in a ritual that centered on the sacrifice of a bull.

Not too much is known about what went on during the remaining days of the festival. On the sixth and seventh days, the god effigies from a number of the major cities of Babylonia were brought to Babylon by road or canal. On the eighth day the king "took Marduk by the hand" and introduced him ceremonially to the visiting gods; then Marduk's sovereignty was solemnly proclaimed by the priests attending the assembled deities. There was a colorful procession headed by Marduk on a sumptuous, jewel-bedecked chariot. Led by the king, who was followed by the visiting gods, this spectacular cortege proceeded from the Esagila, along the impressively decorated Sacred Way, through the Ishtar Gate and out of the city to the *Akitu*-shrine by the Euphrates. The group probably spent three full days there and then returned to the Esagila in Babylon, where the great event of the festival now took place—"the decreeing of the fate" of the king, symbolizing his realm, for the coming year.

Religion undoubtedly played a central role in Mesopotamian life. It was the source and inspiration of magnificent temples, impressive sculpture, decorative steles and plaques, picturesque inlay, attractively engraved cylinder seals. Its rites and rituals were so impressive that they were echoed by most of the ancient world for several millennia. Above all, in that early time when powerful natural forces were utterly inexplicable to fearful humans, their religion gave perspective and order to the lives of the people of Mesopotamia.

# TALES OF GODS
# AND HEROES

*In the elaborate mythology of the*

*Mesopotamian peoples, an array of*

*gods and demigods ruled heaven,*

*earth and the dim netherworld, yet*

*shared the passions and frailties of*

*ordinary men. Among them was the*

*storied Gilgamesh, the half-mortal King*

*of Erech, portrayed at left holding a*

*lion cub as a symbol of his power; he*

*performed many deeds of daring,*

*but he could never achieve his*

*goal of earthly immortality. He*

*did, however, achieve an eternal place*

*in history as did two other heroes of*

*Mesopotamian legend (pages*

*116-117)—the prototypes for the*

*Biblical figures of Noah and Job.*

*Illustrations by Leo and Diane Dillon*

# THE CREATION OF THE UNIVERSE

*According to Sumerian legend, the universe was fashioned out of the primeval sea and divided into heaven and earth by Enlil, god of the air and storms. Here the mighty Enlil is seen separating the heavens, the domain of his father An, from the earth, realm of his mother, the goddess Ki, who is reaching up to him. The Sumerians thought that a great domed roof (below) contained the sky, the stars, the moon and the sun, which lighted the cities beneath it; they also believed that below the earth swirled the dim netherworld, the fearsome abode of demons and the kingdom of the dead.*

# THE BIRTH OF MAN AND BEAST

*The Anunnaki, the divine children of the heaven-god An, were hungry and without*

*clothes, and, the myth says, "knew not the eating of bread [nor] the wearing of*

*garments, ate plants with their mouths like sheep, drank water from the ditch."*

*To provide for them Enlil and Enki, the water-god (whose faces are seen amidst*

*the trees below), created cattle, sheep, plants, the yoke and the plow. But the*

*Anunnaki lacked the skills that were needed to make use of this bounty;*

*it was to tend the sheep and cultivate the fields for these gods*

*that man kneeling at the bottom was fashioned*

*of clay and given breath.*

The gods of Sumer, much like mortal men, suffered the vicissitudes of fate. One of the oft-told tales of Sumerian mythology is that of Inanna, the goddess of love, and her huluppu tree. Inanna, "the always laughing, always rejoicing maid," had found the precious tree on the banks of the Euphrates, and had planted and nurtured it in her garden in the city of Erech, planning to fell it to make a couch and throne for herself. But although the tree grew big, its branches bore no leaves, for "the snake who knows no charm" had wound around its base, the ominous Imdugud bird lived in its crown and in its midst Lilith, the "maid of desolation," had built her house. Here Inanna is seen in front of her huluppu tree, arms upstretched, crying for help. Answering her call, the hero Gilgamesh donned his armor, killed the snake, drove out Lilith and the bird, plucked the tree and "gave it to holy Inanna for her throne." To tempt the gods of

# THE PERILOUS ADVENTURES OF
# AN ANCIENT LOVE GODDESS

*Sumer was risky, even for another god. Inanna nearly lost her life when*

*she descended to the netherworld, trespassing upon the realm of her*

*sister Ereshkigal, the goddess of darkness, gloom and death. Wearing*

*queenly garments and precious jewels, Inanna was admitted to*

*"the land of no return"—then robbed of all her finery as she passed*

*through the seven gates of her sister's palace. Naked and*

*mortified, she was taken before Ereshkigal and seven fierce*

*judges, seen at right, as "they fasten [their] eyes upon*

*her, the eye of death," while she tries to cover her nakedness.*

*Soon their evil glance had done its work, and her*

*corpse was hung from a stake. But Inanna, foreseeing her*

*danger, had instructed her servant Ninshubur to seek*

*help from the gods if she did not return in three days'*

*time; his pleas convinced the god Enki to bring*

*Inanna back to the land of the living. To remain*

*on earth, however, she had to find a replacement*

*for herself in the underworld. Her choice fell*

*on her husband—whom she had found*

*prematurely celebrating her demise*

*—and the gods dispatched*

*him down below to*

*the land of the dead.*

## THE STRANGE ODYSSEY
## OF A MIGHTY KING

The hero Gilgamesh, King of Erech, was strong and handsome, but he oppressed the people of his city and "left no virgin to her lover." When the people begged the gods for help, the gods created Enkidu, a man of untold strength with flowing hair, who roamed the plains and forests with the beasts. Enticed to Erech by a courtesan, Enkidu encountered Gilgamesh, and battled long and fiercely with him (above left). Gilgamesh prevailed, but his fury abated quickly and the two became fast friends. Together, they set out into the world in search of high adventure. As their first feat, they killed Humumba, the fire-breathing guardian of the far-off cedar forest (above).

The odyssey of Gilgamesh and Enkidu continued with their destruction of
the "Bull of Heaven" (above), a beast dispatched to avenge the goddess Ishtar,
whose overtures Gilgamesh had spurned. But the gods decided that Enkidu
must die for murdering the beast. Gilgamesh wept loudly for his friend and
roamed the desert, lamenting, "When I die, shall I not be like unto
Enkidu?" Although part god, he feared that he would have to share the common
lot of man—unless he found the key to immortality. And so he journeyed
to the distant shores where Utnapishtim lived, the only human who enjoyed
eternal life. He passed the Scorpion People who guarded the gate where the
sun rose (top right), and sailed across the sea. At last he reached Utnapishtim,
who told him that to live forever he must fetch the thorny, fragrant plant
of youth from the bottom of the sea. Gilgamesh did so, but during a
moment's inattention on his way home, a snake swallowed the precious
plant (lower right). His quest for immortality had been in vain.

# THE MESOPOTAMIAN ANCESTORS OF NOAH AND JOB

*There was a time when Enlil, the most powerful of the gods, was displeased with mankind and decided to send a flood that no living being could survive. But the verdict seemed too harsh to Ea, a fellow-god, who forewarned his favorite mortal, Utnapishtim, in a dream. Taking heed, Utnapishtim built a boat for himself (left) and loaded it with his family and "the seed of all living creatures . . . the game of the field, and all the craftsmen." The boat weathered the storm, which raged for six days and six nights. On the seventh day, as the waters receded, he disembarked and sent forth his passengers, man and beast. Then, grateful for his survival, he made an offering to the gods, who reproached Enlil for his harsh decision. Enlil, in a gesture of atonement, conferred the gift of immortality upon both Utnapishtim and his devoted wife.*

Among the myths
of Sumer is the story
of an unnamed man,
wealthy, wise and blessed with
family and friends, who found
himself one day alone and ill for
reasons that he was not able to
comprehend. Surrounded by tormentors,
he is seen here at the bottom of the
picture, imploring his guardian god, who is
watching over him. He laments his fate,
crying out, "My righteous word has been
turned into a lie . . . Malignant sickness
bathes my body . . . My god . . . how long will you
neglect me, leave me unprotected?" There is a
happy ending to the story of this Sumerian Job, for
his god heard his prayers and ended his trials as
abruptly as they had begun. But the broader issues
of man's suffering and divine justice—raised
by the Sumerian and still more poignantly by
his Biblical descendant—are with us still.

# 6

# THE LITERATE MAN

Despite the scholarly interest in Classical civilization that flowered during the Renaissance and the Enlightenment, Western man's knowledge of the ancient world was severely limited until the 19th Century. Then not only was the key to hieroglyphic writing found, unlocking the Egyptian past, but the long-standing puzzle of cuneiform script was finally solved—a remarkable feat of scholarship that brought to light lost languages, peoples and cultures and added some 2,000 years of human history to the meager Greek and Biblical sources that alone were available until then.

Primarily responsible for cracking the cuneiform "code" was a young British officer, Henry Creswicke Rawlinson, who in 1835 was assigned as a military adviser to the governor of Kurdistan, a province of Persia. Rawlinson, then 25 years old, was not only a soldier but also a Classical scholar and a student of languages, including Persian. Soon after arriving in the Middle East he became intrigued by the odd, wedge-shaped markings that he observed engraved in stone on a mountain at Ecbatana.

Some time later Rawlinson was drawn to an even more fascinating inscription in the forgotten characters—a huge message engraved on the so-called "Rock of Behistun" in the Zagros Mountains of northwestern Iran. The Rock had been regarded by ancient people as sacred; to them it was known as *Bagistana*, "place of the gods." The great stone formation rose almost perpendicularly 1,700 feet above the little town of Behistun on the ancient caravan road between Babylon and Ecbatana. High on the smooth face, in a seemingly inaccessible spot more than 300 feet above the plain, was carved a huge figure of a man, bow in hand, placing one foot on a defeated rival's neck while other conquered leaders stood nearby. No one knew who the conqueror was, or what his monument meant.

But to Rawlinson, the most challenging feature of the cliff was its gigantic written message, 60 feet wide and 22 feet high. For centuries the wedge-shaped characters had defied efforts to penetrate their mystery; some linguists finally decided that the signs were so bafflingly complex that they would never be deciphered.

Rawlinson was not the first to attack the mystery of cuneiform. In 1765, Carsten Niebuhr, a

mathematician on a Danish expedition, had visited the ruins of the ancient city of Persepolis, where around 500 B.C. the Persian King Darius had built his great palace, later destroyed by Alexander the Great. Niebuhr faithfully prepared accurate copies of several brief inscriptions found on the fallen monuments. He identified three different types of writing inscribed together on the stones; they became known as Old Persian, Elamite, and Akkadian (also called Assyrian or Babylonian).

The first important understanding of the meaning of the strange markings was gained, so one story goes, as a result of a wager in a tavern. In 1802 Georg Friedrich Grotefend, a 27-year-old linguist and teacher of Greek in a German academy, bet some drinking companions that he could figure out the wedge-shaped symbols. With the confidence of youth, Grotefend set to work on inscriptions copied by Niebuhr. The texts included all three types of cuneiform; it was assumed, and later proved true, that the inscriptions were trilingual, that is, the same text had been written in the three different types of cuneiform.

Grotefend concentrated on the upper sections of the Persepolis inscriptions. These parts of the texts had the smallest number of symbols, and he reasoned from their key positions that they must be written in the language of greatest importance,

hence Old Persian. He also figured out from the position and repetition of one sign that it must stand for "king." In addition, he confirmed what had previously been deduced: that another repeated slanting character was simply a divider, grouping characters into words, and that the writing ran from left to right. Through trial and error he began to decipher the separate symbols, and managed to identify ten of the cuneiform signs and three royal names, including that of Darius.

Grotefend had made an inspired start toward deciphering the so-called Class I cuneiform (Old Persian), but he was handicapped by the texts he had to work with; they were far too brief for any real insight into even this relatively simple writing, let alone the far more complex Elamite and Akkadian systems. What was obviously needed was a text of more meaningful length and content.

Some three decades later, Rawlinson encountered the same problem in beginning his own studies. The logical answer was the Rock of Behistun; its inscriptions ran to hundreds of lines, and its text seemed to be repeated in the three systems, side by side. This meant that if one of the classes could be broken, it would provide a key to the other two. Rawlinson was to provide such a key, by copying and translating the markings on the face of the "inaccessible" rock.

Between 1835 and 1847, while not pursuing his military duties, he succeeded in copying the inscriptions on the cliff, often risking his life, once almost losing it. The rock was difficult to climb, simply because it was a sheer vertical face. Around the inscriptions it had been made even more hazardous by the men who had incised the message. They had first smoothed off the surface, filling in holes, cracks and uneven places, and then, after cutting the characters, had coated the finished area with some kind of hard, varnishlike substance that protected the porous limestone. Apparently the ancient craftsmen who made the inscriptions had hacked out temporary paths and erected huge scaffoldings to work on the stone, but these had long since disappeared.

To scale the formidable cliff was a challenge rather than an impossibility to the athletic Rawlinson. Climbing to a ledge, he managed to copy the lowest inscriptions without special equipment. Later he had himself suspended by a rope while he worked; he also used a ladder, balancing it on narrow ledges, while supporting himself perilously atop it as he made copies of the symbols.

The greatest difficulty came in recording the Akkadian script. It was so far out of reach on the vertical face that it thwarted even Rawlinson. To get the work done, he finally hired a native Kurdish boy who inched his way across the smooth surface, somehow clinging to it with his fingers and toes, then supporting himself with ropes attached to wooden wedges he had driven into crevices above the inscriptions. While Rawlinson gave directions from below, the boy made impressions of the script.

As the copies and impressions accumulated, Rawlinson methodically attempted to translate them, starting with the Old Persian. He began his monumental task completely ignorant of Grotefend's previous findings. Working independently of the German schoolmaster, Rawlinson reached virtually the same conclusions, and ultimately went far beyond them.

The message on the Rock of Behistun was, as he suspected, the proclamation of a great conqueror. It was cut into the rock some 500 years before Christ at the order of King Darius himself. Having subdued uprisings in his realm, the victorious ruler used the sacred rock to boast of his greatness, his triumphant campaigns and the extent of his empire. To make sure that his valor did not pass un-

appreciated by any of his subjects, he had the text repeated in three languages used throughout his vast realm: Old Persian, his native tongue; Elamite, spoken by the highland peoples he had conquered in western Persia; and Akkadian, the Semitic language spoken by the Babylonians and Assyrians. The message, now shorn of its mystery after some 2,000 years, includes this command:

> Saith Darius the King:
> Thou who shalt hereafter
> Behold this inscription
> Or these sculptures,
> Do thou not destroy them
> [But] thence onward
> Protect them as long
> As thou shalt be in good strength.

Despite Rawlinson's success in deciphering Old Persian script, many obstacles had to be overcome before the more difficult Elamite and Akkadian systems could be understood. Old Persian had proved relatively simple, consisting of only about 40 symbols, which represented the sounds in the Persian alphabet. But Elamite had over 100 symbols and the Akkadian script consisted of several hundred. Unlike Old Persian, Akkadian was not alphabetic; rather, each sign stood for one or more whole words or syllables. To complicate matters, many cuneiform characters in the latter system could stand for two or more sounds or values.

In spite of these difficulties, the diligent research of a number of scholars finally solved the puzzles of both Elamite and Akkadian; by 1857 all three languages of the Behistun inscription had been deciphered in large part and some of the secrets from the ancient civilizations could now be read.

This newfound ability to understand long-dead languages brought an immediate and surprising result: the first hint of a people and civilization so ancient that all memory of their existence had been lost. Until texts were actually translated, cuneiform was assumed to be of Semitic origin; as far as the early explorers and archeologists knew from their limited Greek and Hebrew sources, only Semitic peoples, related to the people in the Bible, had lived in the land of the Tigris and Euphrates. By 1850, however, a perceptive Protestant Irish clergyman named Edward Hincks had begun to question this assumption, claiming that some of the signs seemed to have non-Semitic characteristics. He was supported by Rawlinson, who pointed out that among the thousands of tablets excavated at Nineveh, many of those he had studied were bilingual and the Semitic Akkadian on the tablets was really nothing more than a translation of a non-Semitic language inscribed beside it.

In 1869 Jules Oppert, a linguist living in Paris, announced that he had figured out the name of the people who had spoken this strange non-Semitic tongue; he had translated an inscription that identified them as a people who lived in a place called Sumer; they had preceded the Akkadians in Mesopotamia, and had originated the cuneiform system of writing later used by their Semitic conquerors.

Thus, the Sumerians as a people first became known to the world. But despite Oppert's deduction, many scholars refused to believe that they had existed. It was not until 1877 when the first large-scale excavations began in southern Mesopotamia, that Oppert was proved right. The earth soon yielded long-buried Sumerian steles, statues, plaques and thousands of clay cones, tablets and fragments inscribed in the Sumerian language. Twelve years later excavations were begun at Nippur, Sumer's cultural center; these have turned up some 30,000 more tablets and fragments.

Sumerian records probably go back to the very beginning of writing. More than a thousand small clay tablets found in Mesopotamia are inscribed with pictographic forerunners of cuneiform script,

dating from about 3100 B.C. The earliest pictographs were basically pictures of objects, often accompanied by symbols that represented numbers; it is clear from the numerals and summations that they were administrative records of cattle, grain and other goods. Later, pictographs came to stand not only for the object pictured but also for certain phonetic sounds. And as pictographic writing developed into cuneiform (see pages 129-137), the foundations of civilized society that rest on written language came into being. Votive objects, such as statues, vases, sacred stones and markers, were inscribed with the donor's name, rank and achievements—the first rudiments of written history. In about 2500 B.C. there begin to appear contracts of land sales and other transactions between private individuals—man's first known legal documents. Some of the writings from this early period are like primers, consisting of long lists of Sumerian words and names; they no doubt were used to teach students, and as such are evidences of the first formal education.

Around 2300 B.C. the Semitic Akkadians, led by Sargon the Great, conquered much of Sumer, and thereafter cuneiform documents written in Akkadian began to multiply. But in the 21st Century B.C. the Sumerian state rose again under the third dynasty of Ur; writing and literature flourished. Sumerian schools became important centers of learning. From this era tens of thousands of documents have been excavated, including the earliest known written code of law, that of the Sumerian King Ur-Nammu.

With the ascendancy of the Babylonian and Assyrian empires during the Second Millennium B.C., the flow of memoranda, inventories and legal records continued. Most of these documents were written in Akkadian, since after a few centuries Sumerian all but vanished as a living tongue. The schools continued to grow and expand. Students and teachers were now Akkadians, but the major part of the curriculum was devoted to the study of Sumerian; in fact, almost all Sumerian literature has reached us through copies made by Akkadian scholars.

By the 15th Century B.C. the flow of cuneiform documents came not only from Mesopotamia, but also from Syria, Palestine and even as far away as Egypt. Many were written in Akkadian, for it was then the international language of the ancient world. But by this time other peoples, such as the Hittites and Hurrians, had borrowed—and occasionally improved upon—the cuneiform script for inscribing their own languages. In Ugarit, a city in Canaanite Palestine, there appeared an alphabetic cuneiform of 30 signs, foreshadowing the arrival of the alphabetic scripts now used throughout the Western world.

One of the greatest discoveries of cuneiform inscriptions was the First Millennium B.C. library of Assurbanipal at Nineveh, the capital of Assyria, excavated in the 1850s by a British archeological team. Its 25,000-odd tablets and fragments are inscribed with bilingual Sumerian-Akkadian texts, literary and religious works, incantations and letters, as well as with diverse astronomical, medical and lexicographical writings. The library was established in the Seventh Century B.C. by the Assyrian King Assurbanipal, who had his scribes copy and collect tablets from all over his kingdom; it remains to this day the most important single collection of cuneiform material ever found. In addition to providing immeasurable help in deciphering and translating the Sumerian and Akkadian languages, it stimulated the search for relics that, archeologists believe, are yet to be found. Although half a million or more cuneiform documents have been excavated over the past century, even this total seems to represent but a small fraction of those that still remain underground.

With the increasing importance of cuneiform writing in the ancient world, the scribe developed into a trained professional. A parable for scribes in Babylon reads: "Writing is the mother of eloquence and the father of artists." Many scribes worked in the temple and the palace, not only as secretaries, bookkeepers and accountants, but also as archivists, recorders and even "writers in residence" who composed hymns or epics on command. Others were employed to help run large estates, while still others were private entrepreneurs, sitting at the city gates, as scribes do to this day in Iraq, waiting for illiterate clients in need of secretarial help. In addition, many went on from their scribal endeavors to become doctors and diviners.

Before a scribe could begin to practice his profession, he had to undergo a long period of education and training in the *edubba*, the Mesopotamian school. Within its walls flourished the scholar and theologian, the linguist and the poet, for the *edubba* was the cultural center of Mesopotamian society.

From archeological findings a good deal is known about these schools—far more, for example, than is known about the Hebrew and Greek schools of a much later day. This knowledge comes mainly from the excavated tablets and records of the *edubba* itself: the professors' textbooks, the students' exercises and amusing essays about school life.

The budding scribe attended school from early youth to young manhood, day after day, month after month, year after year. He had but six days off per month, three holy days and three free days; the remaining school days were—as one ancient graduate noted—"long days indeed." The teaching was monotonous, the discipline harsh. Another former student wrote of a single day in which he was caned at least nine times, his offenses ranging from talking without permission to loitering in the street. His recital of punishments ends on a somewhat less than triumphant note:

*The fellow in charge of Sumerian said:*
*'Why didn't you speak Sumerian?' [He] caned me.*
*My teacher said:*
*'Your hand [writing] is unsatisfactory.' [He]*
*caned me.*
*I [began to] hate the scribal art. . . .*

The students must have been burdened by the many teachers and monitors, watching over them, waiting for some lapse or misdeed that would justify use of the stick. Yet among these harsh disciplinarians there were also professors who were deeply respected and even beloved. One graduate wrote this eulogy of his teacher:

*He guided my hand on the clay, showed me how*
*to behave properly, opened my mouth with*
*words, uttered good counsel, focused [my]*
*eyes on the rules that guide the man of*
*achievement.*

Other boys were less ready to learn, and one father complained bitterly to his son:

*'Where did you go?'*
*'I did not go anywhere.'*
*'If you did not go anywhere, why do you idle*
*about? Go to school . . . Don't stand about in*
*the public square or wander on the boulevard*
*. . . Don't look all around. Be humble and*
*show fear before your monitor. When you show*
*terror, the monitor will like you.'*

The great majority of students attended school regularly to the day of graduation, and, notwithstanding boring exercises and sharp punishments, had reason to be grateful. The *edubba* and its faculty had, after all, turned them into highly respected professionals who were much sought after by their fellow citizens; they were experts qualified to run an estate, arbitrate between contesting parties, survey fields, settle various claims and perform many other essential services.

The most important subject studied was language; students had to master every intricacy of the Sumerian and Akkadian tongues. Beginning with the most elementary syllabic exercises, the neophyte went on to write, read and, as he advanced, to memorize hundreds of cuneiform signs and thousands of Sumerian and Akkadian words and phrases. These were classified by the teachers in "word lists" that became standardized over the centuries; they have been found at virtually every important Mesopotamian site, and even as far afield as Anatolia, Iran and Palestine.

Some of these primers dealt with the natural world, naming hundreds of wild and domestic animals, birds and fish, trees and plants, stones and stars, as well as parts of the human and animal body. Others were geographical primers, containing the names of countries, cities, towns, rivers and canals, and technical primers that itemized innumerable artifacts made of wood, reeds, clay, wool, skin, leather, metal and stone; the wooden objects alone ran into the hundreds, ranging from pieces of raw wood to finished articles such as boats and chariots. Undoubtedly these highly schematic "textbooks" were amplified by explanatory lectures that were never written down, and thus forever lost to posterity.

Mathematics also played an important part in the ancient curriculum. To become a competent secretary, accountant or administrator, a scribe needed a knowledge of arithmetical notation and its practical application. The Mesopotamians commonly used a sexagesimal system—its base was 60, as ours is 10—and like our own decimal system, it made use of place notation so that the position of a numeral in a number indicated its value. The student had to copy and memorize scores of tables for such advanced studies as the calculation of reciprocals, squares and square roots, cubes and cube roots. To explain the operations that were needed

## A NOT SO PROPER SCHOOLMASTER

Like this dignified scribal figure found in Lagash, the teacher-scribes of Sumer's schools were usually models of propriety. But a text written in 2000 B.C. reveals that even the most upstanding teachers occasionally succumbed to flattery.

The story tells of the tribulations of a backward student, who endured frequent canings for tardiness, sloppy dress and poor penmanship. ("My teacher took no delight in me," he lamented.) But what the student lacked in scholarship, he made up in diplomacy. He suggested to his father that the school's headmaster be invited home for dinner. The father complied—and entertained the professor with a lavish feast, gave him a new tunic and slipped him some extra spending money. The professor, overcome by this show of generosity, turned to the student and proclaimed, "You have carried out well the school's activities; you are a man of learning."

for computations, teachers devised sample problems, including some that required the calculations of the areas of fields of different shapes, the number of bricks needed to build a wall and the amount of earth required to build a ramp.

By the time of Hammurabi's reign, about 1750 B.C., a senior student was competent in early forms of algebra and geometry. He knew how to make practical use of what has become known to us as the Pythagorean theorem, although he was not able to prove it theoretically. He also had a fairly accurate idea of the constant quantity we call *pi*, the ratio of the circumference of a circle to its diameter. In order to make calendars, he learned to use astronomical observations such as the rising and setting of Venus and the periodic eclipses of the sun and moon.

By the late First Millennium B.C. an advanced student knew enough mathematical theory to calculate the movement of the planets, and thus was able to advise the king on how to regulate the calendar. The ancient Mesopotamians used a lunar year, made up of 12 lunar months, and every three or four years an extra month was usually inserted in order to keep the calendar synchronized with the solar year.

Since written law played a predominant role in Mesopotamian life, a good part of the school curriculum was devoted to legal studies. The student learned from copies of numerous law codes, written in both the Sumerian and Akkadian languages, as well as large collections of law cases and precedents; he also used sample copies of the different kinds of legal documents in general use and special lists of all the words, phrases and expressions he might meet with during his career.

Medicine was also taught in considerable detail in Mesopotamian schools. Manuals described diagnoses and prognoses for all kinds of illnesses, and gave details of their symptoms and syndromes. There were handbooks listing treatments and remedies, classified according to the part of the body that was afflicted. Drugs were prescribed and administered in potions, salves, poultices and enemas.

Doctors could practice surgery, but this entailed certain risks, at least in the time of Hammurabi. His legal code stated:

*If a surgeon has . . . opened an eye-infection with a bronze instrument and so saved the man's eye, he shall take ten shekels. If a surgeon has . . . opened an eye-infection with a bronze instrument and thereby destroyed the man's eye, they shall cut off his hand.*

In addition to professional physicians and surgeons, another class of healers practiced in ancient Mesopotamia. These medical men were exorcist-priests who relied less on rational treatment than on magic for their cures. They, too, got their training in schools, and the nature of the cures they attempted is suggested by the titles of dozens of manuals they studied, among them "Burning," "Evil Spirits," "All Kinds of Evil," "Deliverances from Curse" and "Headaches." Filled with incantations and rituals of purification, these books purported to relieve suffering from terrors imposed by black magic and possession by devils.

A favorite study in Mesopotamian schools was divination, the art of reading the will of the gods and predicting the future through the interpretation of omens. Almost any occurrence could be interpreted as an omen, good or bad. If, for example, black-winged ants were seen in a town, it was supposed to mean that there would be rain and floods. Another omen inscribed on a clay tablet held: "If an ox has tears in its eyes, some evil will befall the owner of that ox."

Scores of omen manuals were available. One dealt with "messages of the gods" as revealed in the entrails of sacrificial animals; the liver was supposed to be especially significant, and teachers used models of that organ specially prepared for illustration and instruction.

One of the more popular divinatory techniques in Assyrian times was astrology—the art of interpreting the movements and positions of the celestial bodies, as well as such phenomena as thunder, hail and earthquakes. Eventually astrology was used to cast individual horoscopes for people; the Mesopotamians believed, much as many people do today, that a man's future could be foretold from the positions of the planets at the time of his birth.

One subject the Mesopotamian schools neglected was history; instruction in this field was confined primarily to long lists of kings, dynasties and dates. The most important of the historical writings that have survived are the so-called royal annals, accounts of events during a king's reign: invocations to the gods, battles won and new buildings erected; these annals have provided the main sources for the later histories of the ancient Near East.

While history was largely overlooked in the school curriculum, the study of literature received generous attention from the scribes. Over the centuries, poets in particular composed a large and varied body of literary works. Gods were glorified in myths and hymns; heroes were exalted in epic lays. Kings were extolled, or extolled themselves, in rhapsodies like this excerpt from the black obelisk of Shalmaneser III at his palace at Nineveh:

*I am Shalmaneser, King of multitudes of men.*
*Prince and hero of Assur, the strong King,*
*King of all the four zones of the Sun*
*And of multitudes of men.*
*The marcher over the whole world.*

The golden period of Sumerian literature ended with the destruction of Ur in the 21st Century B.C. But even that bitter event had a creative literary result. It gave birth to a "lamentation," a melancholy form of poetry that became a permanent part of Mesopotamian literature, and was later borrowed by the Hebrews. The following work addressed to the goddess Ningal, the wife of the moon-god Nanna, patron god of Ur, is typical of the style:

*O Queen, how has your heart led you on,*
*how can you stay alive! . . .*
    *After your city has been destroyed,*
*how now can you exist! . . .*
    *Your city which has been made into ruins—*
*you are no longer its mistress,*
    *Your righteous house which has been given over to*
*the pickax—you no longer inhabit it,*
    *Your people who have been led to the slaughter—*
*you are no longer their queen.*

Most Mesopotamian literature was poetic in form and was chanted or recited to the accompaniment of musical instruments like the harp, the lyre, the drum and the tambourine. Many poems were written, some apparently for recitation during the "sacred marriages" between Mesopotamian kings and mortal brides who represented the goddess of love. One of the most beautiful of these poems, written some 4,000 years ago, describes the love of a ritual bride of King Shu-Sin. In its imagery it is strikingly reminiscent of the Song of Solomon in the Old Testament:

*Bridegroom, let me caress you,*
*My precious caress is sweeter than honey;*
*In the bed-chamber, honey-filled,*
*Let me enjoy your goodly beauty.*
*Lion, let me caress you.*
*My precious caress is sweeter than honey;*
*Bridegroom, you have taken your pleasure of me;*
*Tell my mother, she will give you delicacies,*
*My father, he will give you gifts.*
*Your spirit, I know where to cheer your spirit;*
*Bridegroom, sleep in our house until dawn,*
*Your heart, I know where to gladden your heart,*
*Lion, sleep in our house until dawn,*
*You, because you love me,*
*Give me, pray, of your caresses,*
*My lord god, my lord protector,*
*My Shu-Sin, who gladdens the heart of Enlil,*
*Give me, pray, of your caresses . . .*

---

## THE WISDOM OF MESOPOTAMIA

The Sumerians and Babylonians summed up their pragmatic views on life with proverbs like those below. The sayings reveal sharp—if not always flattering—insights into the joys and ironies of marriage, riches and human nature in general.

*In a city that has no watch dogs,*
*the fox is the overseer.*

*Who possesses much silver may be happy;*
*who possesses much barley may be glad;*
*but he who has nothing at all may sleep.*

*Flatter a young man, he'll give you anything;*
*Throw a scrap to a dog, he'll wag his tail.*

*The poor men are the silent men in Sumer.*

*Writing is the mother of eloquence*
*and the father of artists.*

*Pay heed to the word of your mother*
*as though it were the word of a god.*

*A sweet word is everybody's friend.*

*Friendship lasts a day, kingship forever.*

*For a man's pleasure there is marriage;*
*on thinking it over, there is divorce.*

*Conceiving is nice; pregnancy is irksome.*

*The wife is a man's future;*
*the son is a man's refuge;*
*the daughter is a man's salvation;*
*the daughter-in-law is a man's devil.*

*If you take the field of an enemy,*
*the enemy will come and take your field.*

*Who builds like a lord, lives like a slave;*
*Who builds like a slave, lives like a lord.*

*Be gentle to your enemy as to an old oven.*

Poets knew nothing of rhyme and meter; their favorite stylistic devices were repetition and parallelism, chorus and refrain, simile and metaphor. Their epic poetry, like that of the Greeks, abounds in long speeches, repetitions and recurrent formulae.

In addition to poetry, Mesopotamians delighted in wise sayings (e.g., "Into an open mouth a fly enters"; "The strong live by their own wages, the weak by the wages of their children") and in so-called "wisdom literature." An example of the latter is the "Poem of the Righteous Sufferer," which deals with a man seemingly forsaken by the gods, like the Biblical Job. The man, who is given no name, speculates on the frailties of men and the changeability of fate:

> Who came to life yesterday, died today.
> In but a moment man is cast into gloom,
>   suddenly crushed.
> One moment he will sing for joy,
> And in an instant he will wail—a mourner.
> Between morning and nightfall men's mood
>   may change:
> When they are hungry they become like corpses,
> When they are full they will rival their god,
> When things go well they will prate of rising up to
>   heaven.
> And when in trouble, rant about descending into Hell.

From the time of Hammurabi, or even earlier, most literary works were written in Akkadian; but the form and content, the themes and motifs, the style, even the names of characters and protagonists, were those of Sumerian times. The Akkadian *Epic of Gilgamesh*, Mesopotamia's major contribution to world literature, is an outstanding example of this elaboration of Sumerian literature. The poem, some 3,500 lines long, describes the life of Gilgamesh, an early ruler of Erech, from his arrogant youthful days as an oppressive tyrant to his chastened return as a frustrated wanderer over land and sea *(see pages 109-117)*. It is a grand and moving tale, concerned with universal problems of loyalty, courage and man's timeless thirst for immortality.

The Epic sings of the strong friendship between Gilgamesh and the wild man Enkidu; of their adventurous expedition to the magic, monster-guarded cedar forests; of Gilgamesh's bold defiance of the goddess of love; of the two men's struggle with the "Bull of Heaven" sent down to punish them for this indiscretion; of Enkidu's death and Gilgamesh's quest for eternal life; of his visit to Utnapishtim, the flood-hero and prototype of Noah—a venture that ended in failure when Gilgamesh learned that immortality cannot be attained by men.

Almost all of the episodes in the Epic are taken from older Sumerian tales and even the story of Utnapishtim has its Sumerian counterpart. The Akkadians did not, however, copy the Sumerian tales slavishly, but they modified and molded them into a closely knit and forceful drama—something that Sumerian bards were apparently unable to achieve. A sample of the Epic's style is seen in this excerpt, in which an innkeeper along Gilgamesh's route discourages him in his quest for unending life —a futile quest that recurs frequently as a theme in Mesopotamian literature:

> Gilgamesh, whither are you wandering?
> Life, which you look for, you will never find.
> For when the gods created man, they let
> Death be his share, and withheld life
> In their own hands.
> Gilgamesh, fill your belly—
> Day and night make merry,
> Let days be full of joy.
> Dance and make music day and night,
> And wear fresh clothes.
> And wash your head and bathe.
> Look at the child that is holding your hand,
> And let your wife delight in your embrace.
> These things alone are the concern of men.

# HOW WRITING BEGAN

More than any other achievement, the invention of writing brought the luster of civilization to the lives of men. Taking this giant step more than 5,000 years ago made it possible to preserve thoughts and experiences, and to hand down hard-won wisdom to future generations—two processes essential for the maintenance of a complex society. The first written words were pictographs used by the Sumerians to record inventories. As time went on, scribes refined these crude symbols into a complex script capable of expressing abstract ideas. So elaborate did this script become, employing more than 700 different signs, that years of study were required to learn it, and scribes became educated professionals who often held high office.

ASSYRIAN SCRIBES, *shown in a bas-relief from a palace at Nimrud, make lists of captured booty as the items are counted off by an official (left).*

129

THE SIGN FOR "OX" began as a stylized picture of an ox's head, as shown on the tablet above. Soon scribes found they could write lists more easily by turning the tablet and marking each sign sideways (right). Eventually, the sign was simply written on its side with five wedge-shaped marks (above right).

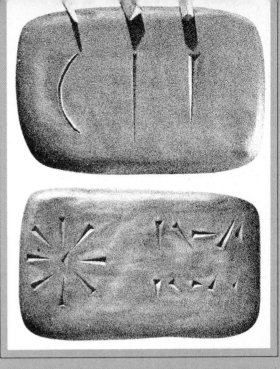

STROKES OF TABLETS *were originally made by scratching with a pointed stylus (near right). Later, the marks were formed by pressing a triangular stylus into the damp clay (center). Finally, the stylus became blunter and its mark more clearly wedge-shaped (far right).*

THE RANGE OF MARKS *possible using a stylus with a wedge-shaped tip is shown by a star pattern. But in practice scribes found that they could make only half these—the long and short impressions shown at far right— without changing their grip on the stylus.*

# SHAPING THE WRITTEN SYMBOL

Writing evolved in Mesopotamia out of a practical need to keep records. The earliest known examples of written Sumerian, dating from about 3100 B.C., are marks on small tablets that were attached like shipping tags to sacks of grain and other agricultural products. The tags were engraved with simplified drawings known as pictographs, which recorded the quantity and type of material the sacks contained. Wealthy Sumerians who owned large storehouses of grain and herds of livestock used bigger tablets inscribed with columns of pictographs to keep accounts.

Practical considerations also determined the tools and shaped the symbols of writing. Tablets were made from clay, the most plentiful raw material in Mesopotamia. A reed stylus, whittled to a sharp point, was used to produce the fine, curving lines of the early pictographs. These were carefully set down on vertical columns, beginning at the top right-hand corner of each tablet.

Early in the Third Millennium B.C., Sumerian scribes began to change this technique in order to write more quickly and legibly. By turning the tablets and writing in horizontal rows, they avoided smudging the text with their hands—an annoying hazard when writing in vertical columns; as a result, the pictographs appeared sideways and read from left to right, top to bottom. The pointed stylus, which left messy ridges in the damp clay, was discarded in favor of a stylus with a triangular tip, which was pushed down into the clay rather than drawn across it, leaving a series of quick, wedge-shaped impressions.

With these innovations, the character of the pictographs changed; no longer drawings of objects, they evolved into abstract symbols, a kind of early shorthand. These made up the writing system known as cuneiform (from the Latin word for "wedge-shaped"), which characterized the culture of Mesopotamia for the next 2,500 years.

# FROM PICTOGRAPH INTO SCRIPT

The first picture writing suffered from several built-in limitations. While simple pictographs sufficed to represent objects—a drawing of a head simply meant "head"—they were unable to express more abstract words, such as the verb "to think." Consequently, the scribes began to use pictographs as ideograms, symbols similar to modern Chinese characters that stood for several related words or concepts. For example, the sign meaning "mouth" *(right)* was also used for the verb "to speak." Occasionally, this practice led to ambiguities, as with the symbol for "foot," which meant both "to stand" and "to go."

The final step in the development of cuneiform occurred when scribes began using symbols phonetically, to indicate sounds as well as ideas. The Sumerian word for "arrow," pronounced *ti*, was the same as the word for "life." So the scribes used the same sign, a picture of an arrow, to write both words. By giving each sound a phonetic symbol, it was possible to spell out any word in the language. (Using the same method in English, the word "season" would be represented by pictures of the sea and the sun). The use of phonetic symbols gave writing such flexibility that the later Akkadians, Babylonians and Assyrians were able to adapt cuneiform to inscribe their own quite different tongues.

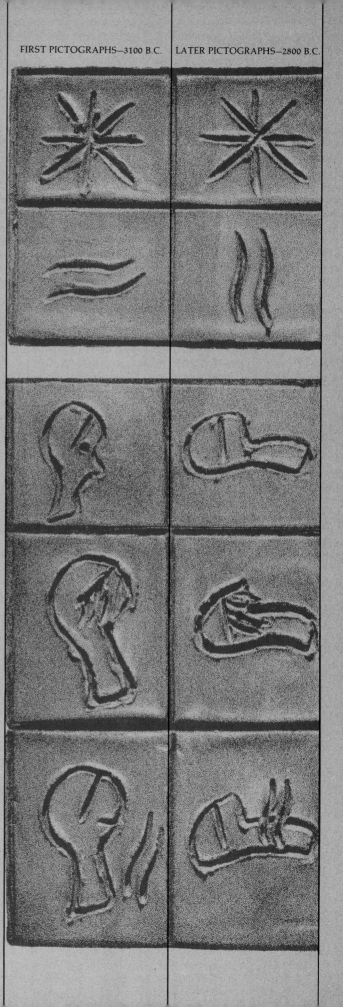

EARLY CUNEIFORMS—2500 B.C.          OLD BABYLONIAN—1800 B.C.          ASSYRIAN—700 B.C.

THE SIGN FOR "STAR" *evolved over the centuries from a drawing (far left) into a more abstract symbol (right). It also stood for the words "heaven" and "god" in both the Sumerian and Assyrian tongues.*

SYMBOL OF A SOUND, *the wavy lines at far left represented the Sumerian word "a," meaning "water." Since the word for "in" was also "a," the symbol, which grew more stylized, was used to write "in."*

COMPOSITE SYMBOLS *added flexibility to writing by giving new meanings to basic pictographs. Extra lines on the pictograph for "head" (top row, far left) produced the symbol for "mouth" (middle row). Combining the mouth symbol with the sign for "water" resulted in an ideogram that meant "to drink" (bottom row). All three symbols developed in the same manner. They began as pictographs (far left), which were turned sideways, and later inscribed with wedge-shaped strokes. In their final form, in Assyrian times, most strokes were made either horizontally or vertically for the sake of clarity.*

133

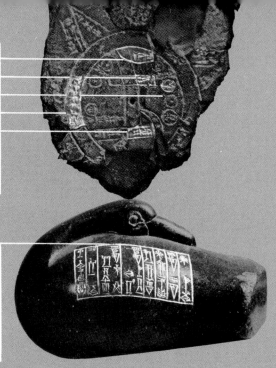

MOUNTAIN
CITY OF BABYLON
ASSYRIA
BITTER RIVER
REED THICKET

A Babylonian map, giving a highly stylized view of the world, was drawn about 600 B.C. and marked with cuneiform place names.

FOR NANNA, HIS MASTER, THE MIGHTY . . . KING OF UR, KING OF THE FOUR QUARTERS, CONFIRMS FIVE MINAS

A stone weight of about five pounds was dedicated to the god Nanna by a local king.

ABOVE THE TERRACE OF SHAGARAKII-SHURLASH, SON OF KUDUR-ENLIL, I LAID ITS FOUNDATIONS AND SET FIRMLY ITS BRICKWORK

A cylindrical tablet honors the rebuilding of a temple erected by a Babylonian king.

GODDESS ISHTAR IS VOWED

A votive figure, carved in stone some 46 centuries ago, was inscribed for Idi-Narum, an official at the Temple of Ishtar.

**25 LOAVES—20 BARLEY CAKES**

*A commercial record, inscribed on a clay tablet in the Third Millennium B.C., lists various quantities of food and other goods.*

**PULVERIZE PEARS AND THE ROOTS OF THE MANNA PLANT: PUT IN BEER AND LET THE MAN DRINK**

*A medical text, shown slightly larger than actual size, describes pharmaceutical preparations made from Sumerian plants and herbs.*

# THE MANY USES OF CUNEIFORM

As writing grew more and more versatile, its role expanded in the culture of Mesopotamia. No longer limited to recording concrete objects, it could be used to develop a whole literature of religious, technical and historical documents, comprising millions of tablets, six of which are shown here with partial translations. To the early inventories of agricultural goods were added astronomical tables, law codes, medical texts and literary chronicles. New materials were pressed into use. Words were chiseled into stone, painted onto pottery and engraved on wax-coated panels.

Writing began to take on ceremonial and even magical qualities. A tablet addressed to one of the Mesopotamian gods was set into the foundations of temples and palaces, and many people wore engraved amulets designed to ward off evil spirits. The Babylonians and Assyrians held the written word in such awe that they believed their destinies were shaped by it; death came, they felt, when a divine scribe etched their names in a mythical Book of Fate.

DARIUS THE GREAT

# A KING'S WORDS

The most famous—and the most awesome
—of all cuneiform inscriptions is a proclamation hewn 340 feet above the ground,
into the face of a mountain at Behistun,
Iran. Commissioned some 2,500 years ago
by Darius the Great, King of Persia, it
describes the military triumphs by which
Darius secured his throne. The bas-relief
that adjoins the message shows the Persian monarch, portrayed life-size, receiving as prisoners 10 vanquished rivals.

Behistun's fame rests on the fact that
its 1,306 lines of weather-beaten script
provided the key that enabled 19th Century scholars to decipher cuneiform. To
make his words intelligible throughout his
domain, Darius had the inscription carved
in three languages: his native Old Persian,
Akkadian and Elamite. The scholars managed to puzzle out the sense of parts of
Old Persian, and then, by comparing the
three texts, to decipher the Akkadian and
Elamite. This success cracked the "code"
of the thousands of cuneiform tablets unearthed from the sands of Mesopotamia.

# 7
# THE BEAUTIFUL, THE PRACTICAL

Mesopotamia, especially in its southern half, is hardly outstanding for the wealth of its natural resources. Water and mud are its principal assets. Yet in spite of this, or perhaps because of it, the ancient Mesopotamians invented the fundamental tools and techniques that support modern civilization. In the course of doing so they not only satisfied their immediate needs for food, clothing and shelter; they also created a new life style, one less urgently concerned with survival. With more leisure time for higher pursuits, they were free to satisfy other needs for the beautiful and the holy. From the first hesitant scratchings of decorative motifs on utilitarian objects they went on to develop fine arts and monumental architecture that rank among the earliest and greatest of man's esthetic achievements.

The inspiration for this developing esthetic sense was, by and large, religious, and nowhere is it easier to trace than in the emerging form of the temple in Mesopotamia. This country's temples and shrines are the forerunners of the synagogue, the church, the cathedral and the mosque. And it was the birthplace of the idea that man has a sacred duty to build his god a home. Almost as soon as he had settled down and learned to build a house for himself, the Mesopotamian provided a similar house for his god.

The first of these primitive shrines must have been very like the one uncovered in the excavations at Eridu. Lying beneath 17 layers of later civilization, and only a few layers above the earliest signs of human habitation, there is a small structure obviously meant for a religious purpose. It dates from sometime between 5000 B.C. and 4000 B.C., and contains only one room, measuring about 12 by 15 feet. In its center there is an offering table and on one wall a niche for the cult object. The plan of the shrine is open and the doorway is wide, inviting the worshiper to enter at will and move about freely. Whatever the ritual performed there, it probably did not involve an official priesthood; man communicated directly with his god.

Four hundred miles to the north of Eridu, at Tepe Gawra, archeologists have unearthed several other religious structures similar in plan to the shrine at Eridu. Apparently certain features of the

A DECORATIVE PLAQUE, *unearthed at Ur, is inlaid with mythological figures that exemplify the skilled artistry of Mesopotamia's craftsmen. The figures, made of shell against a lapis lazuli background, show, from the top, the legendary hero Gilgamesh wrestling with two bulls, various animals carrying food and playing music, and a scorpion-bodied man with a gazelle (last row).*

Mesopotamian temple—namely the niche and the offering table—had already become standardized. One of the major finds at Tepe Gawra, a temple recovered almost completely intact, contributes another of these features. The temple, called the Northern Temple, is one of three; it is arranged in an unusual U-shaped cluster, and dates from about 3500 B.C. Although still very modest in size, the Northern Temple foreshadows the later greater temples of Mesopotamia. The walls are buttressed at regular intervals, inside and out, with brick pilasters. Undoubtedly they were intended to strengthen the walls, but they were also clearly directed at something beyond mere utility. The buttresses pattern the walls with bays and recesses, giving them a surface texture and a sense of form —the beginnings of architectural monumentality.

Despite this sophistication of form, the Northern Temple is still open in plan, consisting essentially of only one room; the purpose of the temple was still uncomplicated—and so was the pattern of man's communication with his god. Elsewhere this was no longer true. At Eridu there is a second temple, at a level dated 1,000 years later than that of the first small shrine at the same site. Like Tepe Gawra, its walls are deeply buttressed and recessed, but unlike Tepe Gawra, its interior is divided: a long, narrow central hall is surrounded by a series of smaller chambers. The temple had become more complex. It was no longer simply a sanctuary, but had taken on the added functions of warehouse and administrative center; the little rooms are storerooms and offices.

As the activities of the community became more involved, the temple was expanded to accommodate them, for the temple was the center of community life—economic and political, as well as religious. To the Mesopotamian, this arrangement was entirely logical. Man existed solely to serve the god, and therefore all of man's activities were properly regulated from the god's house. Apart from its more elaborate plan, this temple at Eridu is also significant for its site. It rests upon a terrace reached by climbing a flight of stairs—the first instance of a shrine being raised above the level of the surrounding houses.

In another ancient Mesopotamian city, Erech, the god's house became an impressive edifice very early. Erech is renowned for its grand temples. Among them, dating from about 3200 B.C., are two placed at right angles to each other, and probably dedicated to the god An and the goddess Inanna. Between the two temples is a courtyard in which the customarily dun-colored clay walls are decorated with a colorful zigzag mosaic. The individual tiles are actually clay cones, in black, white and red, inserted into the walls so that only their round bases protrude. On one side the courtyard rises to a terrace, culminating in a row of massive columns decorated with the same cone mosaics.

At a somewhat later date this temple complex was filled in, courtyard and all, and a second group of three temples was built on top. Two of these, probably dedicated to the goddess Inanna, lay at right angles to each other; the third, set apart from them, was a temple to An and is commonly called the White Temple for its white-washed walls. The White Temple sits on an artificial mound 40 feet high—no doubt the debris of some earlier structure that the builders did not bother to clear away. Nevertheless it is one of the first foreshadowings of the ziggurat, the massive step-sided tower that later became such a dominant feature of the Mesopotamian landscape. Its plan, a central hall flanked by side rooms, is one that had now become predominant all over Mesopotamia.

But within the norm there were many variations. Near Tell Uqair, for example, an ancient town not far from modern Baghdad, there is a temple decorated with a painted frieze of human and animal figures. At Eshnunna, near the Diyala River, several temples have sanctuaries approached through a vestibule and forecourt, while several others have walls so thick that archeologists think they may have supported some sort of barrel vaulting. And from the debris of one small temple at Ur, Sir Leonard Woolley has extracted and reassembled the bits and pieces of several mosaic-covered columns, as well as some copper bas-reliefs and copper statues of bulls.

The debris of this little temple also yielded another important discovery: a small, rather crudely lettered limestone tablet containing the brief statement, "A-anne-pad-da, king of Ur, the son of Mes-anni-pad-da, king of Ur, has built the house for his Nin-Kharshag [the Sumerian mother goddess Ninhursag]." The tablet confirms the existence of a king, Mes-anni-pad-da, whose name appears on the king lists of later scribes, but who was long thought by some scholars to be a figment of the Sumerian imagination. And since the king lists are written in chronological order, the tablet provides a clue not only to the date of the shrine, but to all the other objects found at the site. It also confirms that temple building had become, by the middle of the Third Millennium, a prerogative of kings rather than the joint enterprise of a whole community.

One of the best descriptions of a royal temple building comes from two large clay cylinders found at Lagash, 25 miles north of Ur. They tell of a temple built by Gudea, the king of Lagash, in about 2100 B.C. for the god Ningirsu. Gudea purified his city with prayers and sacrifices before and after building the temple, and when it was completed staffed it with a group of minor deities—much as one would staff an estate. Among them were the supernatural equivalents of a doorkeeper, a butler, two armorers, a messenger, a chamberlain, a coachman, a goatherd, two musicians, four grain and fish inspectors, a gamekeeper and a bailiff. Unfor-

tunately, very little of this temple has been found, but it probably resembled the Ekishnugal found at Ur, dating from the same period, which includes a ziggurat and a number of shrines, along with storehouses, courts and dwellings for the temple personnel.

For the last 2,000 years of ancient Mesopotamian history, the temple itself was less impressive than the ziggurat of which it was a part. Physically, the ziggurat—a stepped brick tower with a small shrine on the summit—is related to the pyramid. Spiritually the two are poles apart. The pyramid is a sunless labyrinthine tomb; the ziggurat is a sunbathed ladder for the god, connecting earth and heaven. Like so many of man's creations, it came into being inadvertently. As new temples were built upon the ruins of the old ones, and the terraces of each successive building climbed higher, some of the more imaginative Sumerian priests must have been struck by the resemblance to steps, and found the idea appealing. Whatever the reason, over the centuries the terracing became deliberate. Each terrace was smaller than the one below, in height as well as size, and was connected to it by a monumental staircase. The towers, at their highest, climbed into the sky as much as 290 feet; the base terrace was often a huge manmade plateau, hundreds of feet on a side and five times the height of a man. In plan, the ziggurat was square or rectangular, circular or oval; in profile it rose anywhere from one to seven stages.

To date, archeologists have unearthed the remains of more than 30 ziggurats, scattered all over Mesopotamia. The most famous one, historically, is the Etemenanki at Babylon, which some scholars believe may be the Biblical "Tower of Babel." Today nothing is left of the Etemenanki except its foundations. But Herodotus, the Greek historian who visited Babylon and saw the ziggurat in the Fifth Century B.C., described it as a splendid affair of seven levels, or stages, each faced with a different color of baked brick. At the top was a shrine of blue-enameled brickwork, furnished inside with a large comfortable couch and a table of gold for the use of the god when he came down to earth.

Far more is known about another, much more complete ziggurat excavated at Ur by Leonard Woolley. The Ur ziggurat dates from about the 21st Century B.C., and was built during the reign of two Sumerian kings, Ur-Nammu and Shulgi. It is a solid, three-stage tower with a core of mud brick and a façade of baked brick set in bitumen—a natural asphalt found in surface beds in various parts of Mesopotamia. The bottom stage of the ziggurat is about 50 feet high and covers an area roughly 150 by 200 feet; each of the two upper stages is correspondingly smaller in size, leaving a broad walkway at each level. On three sides the walls of the ziggurat rise sheer to the terrace above. On the fourth, a series of stairways connect each stage and presumably led to a temple at the summit—of which nothing remains. From time to time over the centuries this ziggurat fell into ruins and was repaired by one or another pious ruler of Assyria or Babylonia. Its last royal patron was Nabonidus, a king who reigned over Babylon in the Sixth Century B.C. and who transformed the ancient Sumerian relic into an impressive seven-stage tower.

With the rise of the empire-building Assyrians, temples lost some of their significance and became mere appendages of the palaces. The gods were not the only force that regulated Mesopotamian life; men's fate was also being determined by the king and his conquering army. The shrines, to be sure, were still large and numerous, and the ziggurats were lofty as ever. But the temple, as an administrative center, was being replaced by the palace—and with this change the palace became the object of greater architectural interest.

In Assur, for instance, the ancient capital of As-

syria, the temple had stood alone on its acropolis, the uncontested center of the city's life. But by the time Assur was replaced by Calah as the capital of the Assyrian Empire, in 879 B.C., the temples of that city's various gods had to share the acropolis with the royal palace, and in fact were adjuncts to it. Even the famous Nebuchadrezzar II of Babylon, for all his respect for the gods, made the great temple to Marduk part of the palace enclosure by joining the two with an elaborate Processional Way.

The royal palaces, which were to develop into huge complexes of legendary grandeur and luxury, had simple enough origins. The two oldest uncovered so far are at Eridu and Kish. Both date from about 2700 B.C. and resemble other buildings of their period, except for their more numerous compartments. But by 2000 B.C., the palace had begun to acquire a distinctive architectural character. At Eshnunna, the palace of the governors contained a throne room and the beginnings of a processional way—the route to the throne room lay along a paved brick path that cut diagonally through an open courtyard. The Eshnunna palace also contained a small shrine, presumably a sort of royal chapel for the ruler's private devotions.

By the time of the great Hammurabi, around 1800 B.C., the royal dwelling had become a truly imposing affair. One of the largest and most magnificent palaces in all of Mesopotamia belonged to a contemporary of Hammurabi, a king named Zimrilim whose capital was the city of Mari, in what is now Syria. Zimrilim's palace had an immense courtyard, paved in alabaster. Another small courtyard, its walls covered with painted frescoes of gods, goddesses and battles, set off the throne room from several temples and shrines. In addition there were literally hundreds of rooms and apartments for the king and his family, for court officials, guards, servants and visiting guests.

Grand as it was, Zimrilim's palace could not

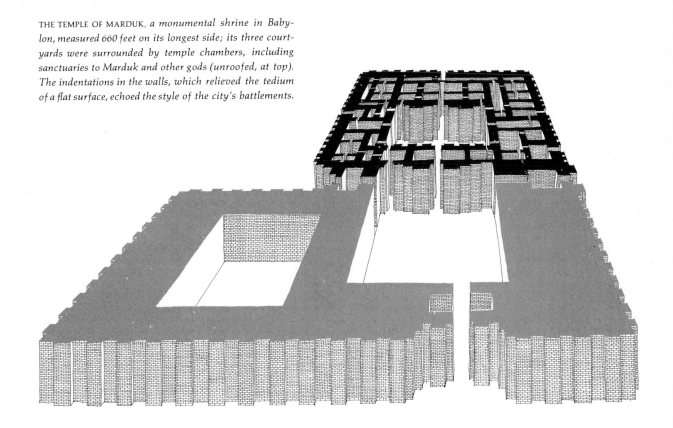

THE TEMPLE OF MARDUK, *a monumental shrine in Baby-lon, measured 660 feet on its longest side; its three court-yards were surrounded by temple chambers, including sanctuaries to Marduk and other gods (unroofed, at top). The indentations in the walls, which relieved the tedium of a flat surface, echoed the style of the city's battlements.*

compare with those of later kings of Assyria and Babylonia. The palaces of Sargon II at Dur-Shar-rukim and of his son and great-grandson, Sennach-erib and Assurbanipal, at Nineveh, were enormous citadels. Sitting astride the city walls on massive platforms of earth, they formed, together with their temples and ziggurats, a complex of royal build-ings worthy of the warrior-kings who built them. Among the most notable elements of these for-tress palaces were the colossal statues of winged, human-headed bulls that guarded their portals, and the sculptured reliefs that lined their interior walls. The bull statues were often carved of single blocks of alabaster, 10 to 15 feet high. The reliefs, also carved from stone, were picture stories that told in minute and sometimes monotonous detail of the king's military exploits—all of which invaria-bly ended in disaster for his foes.

By the time of Sargon, these statues and reliefs represented one of Mesopotamia's major artistic achievements, and, like architecture, their chief function was to impress ordinary men with the power and glory of the king. But sculpture too had grown from an essentially religious origin. The first statues and stone carvings, dating from the late Fourth Millennium, had been associated with the temple and with the rites of worship.

Among the most important of the first works in this field is a group of figures-in-the-round, called "praying statues," found at Tell Asmar.

These figurines served a curious purpose. The Mesopotamians believed that in order to achieve a long and prosperous life constant prayers to the gods were imperative. But such piety was often im-practical. To circumvent the onerous task, some in-genious priest conceived the notion of creating a stand-in, a stone statue that could be left in front of the altar permanently in an attitude of prayer.

The earliest "praying statues" of Tell Asmar, de-spite the crudity of their workmanship, are ex-traordinary works of art. The intensity of their gaze, fixed and hypnotic, and the humility of their folded hands express deep religious conviction. At the same time there is a forcefulness to their stance and a firmness to their pursed lips that is indicative of a demand for divine recognition. The statues are at once worshipful and self-assertive.

It is astonishing that in a region so short of stone a sculptural style of such technical proficiency and daring should develop. Even these very early "praying statues" are modeled, consciously or unconsciously, according to an artistic convention. The eyes are grossly exaggerated in size, yet never grotesque. The bodies are elongated and certain features—beards, muscles, folds of clothing—have been handled as geometrical abstractions. Later on, the details of the human body were rendered more naturalistically. These later figures were often inlaid with gold or highlighted with pigment, and some of them were cast from bronze or copper instead of being carved from stone. The last great flowering of sculpture-in-the-round was at Lagash during the reign of Gudea, about 2100 B.C. Although Lagash at the time was almost surrounded by hostile forces from the east, none of the uncertainty created by this danger is apparent in the city's art. Indeed, the sculptors of Lagash were producing statues of their king that are remarkable chiefly for their tranquility.

After Lagash, sculpture-in-the-round declined but bas-relief did not. Indeed, some of the finest reliefs were carved for the powerful Assyrian kings during the last great days of the Mesopotamian civilization before its decline. But these late reliefs, for all their skill, lack certain qualities present in the earliest work. The first bas-reliefs, like the first statues, were more vivacious in spirit. Some are carved with such exuberance that the figures seem to pop right out of their background, while in others the liveliness is a matter of line—they are like finely drawn etchings.

One of the best of these early reliefs is on an alabaster vase found among the ruins of a temple at Erech. Probably meant for some ceremonial use, it is about three feet tall and is banded with three rows of figures that, taken together, illustrate one of the city's sacred festivals. At the bottom is a band of animals and grain, then comes a band of men bearing gifts, and finally, at the top, there is a scene of the goddess receiving men's offerings. Although all of the figures on the vase are parts of a unified design, each also has a character of its own, a distinct identity.

As time went on, relief carving, like other kinds of art, became identified with activities of kings. Sometime during the 24th Century B.C., Naram-Sin, the grandson of Sargon, commissioned the carving of a plaque, or stele, commemorating a great victory. Naram-Sin's stele depicts a battle in the mountains, and is unusual in its composition. Instead of telling the story in a series of horizontal bands, the sculptor arranged his figures diagonally along the side of a mountain, with the king's figure at the top. It is a much more unified composition, and more dynamic; everything builds to the king.

During the reign of the great Assyrian kings, artists outdid themselves to report in stone the exploits of their rulers—on the battlefield, in the palace and at the hunt. These late reliefs are done with enormous skill and are full of fascinating detail. It is possible to see exactly how a chariot looked or what constituted a soldier's armor. But the artist is no longer expressing his own individual ideas about his subjects; he is following an artistic convention —his kings and soldiers and servants are stereotypes. Only the animals are portrayed with any freedom —a wounded lion collapses in anguish, or a mare shows tender concern for her foal. It is as though human events had become too formalized to be treated as spontaneous occurrences.

In the minor arts this preoccupation with convention is much less true, and the artist's imagination had much freer rein. Two of these minor arts are especially appealing artistically—and revealing of Mesopotamian life. One is the art of inlay, in which small bits of shell and colored stone are set into bitumen, a technique used mainly for ornamenting objects meant for household or personal use—little boxes, gameboards, musical instruments. The other was the art of carving stone cylinder seals. These small objects, engraved with the owner's personal symbol or signature, rolled their way all over the ancient world as a sort of trademark on documents and other objects of value. The cylinder seal was in continuous use for 3,000 years, and is found at every archeological site. It is therefore a record of the habits and activities of kings and common people, and of the changing attitudes toward art and technical craftsmanship.

The very earliest seals are engraved with simple figures and scenes—mythical creatures, kings and heroes, shepherds protecting their flocks. Gradually these scenes were replaced by stylized patterns that created, in repeat, an engraved "brocade." One of the most popular subjects for seal-cutters in southern Mesopotamia was a scene in which a man (presumably the seal's owner) is presented to a god by another god, probably the owner's "guardian angel." In the north, in Assyria, seal-cutters developed a whole repertoire of subjects and styles; some are heraldic motifs, some are scenes of animals in combat, some illustrate stories of the gods.

All the Mesopotamians' highly developed arts, from seal-cutting to sculpture and architecture, rested on a broad foundation of skilled craftsmanship. These ancient peoples were able to create many things of great beauty because they had first learned how to make humbler things of great utility. They invented the tools and techniques that made their country the first in the world to enjoy the security of a life based on large-scale agriculture. They became talented bakers, brewers and

weavers. Their bricks and tiles were so well made that many have lasted for 5,000 years. And they were the first to master exceedingly delicate processes of metallurgy.

In some aspects, Mesopotamian crafts were surprisingly sophisticated. Farmers, for example, used a seeder-plow, a device that not only turned the ground but also dropped seeds into the new furrow through a funnel-like attachment. Far simpler but far more versatile was the Mesopotamian pickax, a kind of short-handled hoe. Unlike the plow, which worked only four months of the year, the pickax labored all year round. It dug canals and built dams to irrigate fields and meadows; it drained flooded land and prepared the soil for plowing; it built mud-walled houses, and stalls for cattle and sheep; it mended city streets and built city walls. So cherished was the pickax that the ancient Sumerians considered it a gift from the gods, given, says one epic, "to the black headed people to hold."

Some of the pickax's most useful work was in the care of the gardens and palm groves that provided the Mesopotamian not only with his daily food but also with a multitude of by-products. From barley, which was grown as the staple crop in preference to wheat, he ground flour for an unleavened bread or extracted malt for beer—a beverage that Sumerian poets described as bringing "joy to the heart" and "happiness to the liver." From sesame seed he pressed sesame oil for cooking, and from flax he got fine fibers that he combed, wove and dyed into excellent linen cloth.

Some of the Mesopotamian farmer's most important skills were associated with the processing of materials he got from his farm animals. Their skins were tanned by soaking them in a solution of alum and gallnut, then rubbed with fats and oils to make them supple. From the leather, the Mesopotamian made shoes and sandals, harnesses and saddles, bags and waterbottles. Goat hair was used extensively for carpets, and sheep's wool was the foundation of a textile industry that was a rich source of foreign commerce. The wool was sometimes spun into thread and woven on looms, sometimes made into felt.

The Mesopotamians also acquired a good deal of knowledge about the practical chemistry of metals, especially of copper and bronze. The metalsmith was in fact one of the more important craftsmen of Sumer. He imported his copper ore from Asia Minor and tin ore from the Caucasus Mountains, and smelted utilitarian bronze directly from a mixture of the two ores. Later, he produced a purer product by mixing metallic copper and tin that he had first smelted separately from their ores. For smelting and casting, the smith used a special furnace, crucibles of earthenware or metal, and a leather bellows. The molten metal was cast into either flat, open molds or three-dimensional closed molds. Some richly detailed castings were even produced by the complicated "lost-wax" method, in which the original matrix was modeled in wax, then coated with clay, after which the wax was melted away to leave its design in the inner surface of the clay. The smith also strengthened his metals by annealing, and joined parts by soldering and riveting.

Closely related to the metalsmith was the craftsman who worked in gold and silver and semi-precious stones. He too knew how to cast metal in molds—sometimes in multi-part molds of three and four pieces. He also had at his command other forming techniques: he knew how to spin gold and silver into threads for filigree and how to stamp flat pieces with a surface pattern. He had even mastered the art of beating metal into paper-thin sheets, which he then shaped into three-dimensional objects by hammering them over wooden cores. In much of his work, he had a partner, the lapidary, a man who made beads, bracelets and pendants from such things as pearls and precious stones.

It was probably these lapidaries, experimenting with sand, quartz, soda and lime who inadvertently discovered the process for making glazes and glass. Mesopotamians knew about glassmaking as early as 2500 B.C., and by 1700 B.C. an enterprising craftsman had written down the recipes, perhaps for his own files, perhaps for posterity. If his purpose was the latter, he succeeded beyond his wildest dreams, for in the mid-20th Century A.D. two British glassmakers used one of his recipes to make two small vessels, now in the British Museum.

Mesopotamia also had other skilled craftsmen—carpenters whose tools included hammers, chisels, saws and drills, and whose products ranged from furniture to ships; basketmakers who turned the tall, strong marsh reeds into containers of every sort as well as into fences and huts.

But the artisan whose product had the most far-reaching effect upon his own and later civilizations was the man who manipulated wet clay—the humble, fragile, all-purpose material of ancient life. One of these craftsmen in clay was the potter, who learned very early to construct and fire his kiln, as well as to burnish and decorate his indispensable ware with colorful designs; by 3500 B.C. he had begun to use the potter's wheel and was turning out his product on a mass-production basis. Meanwhile, his fellow craftsman, the brickmaker, was providing the material for monumental architecture by packing muddy clay into wooden forms and baking it either in the sun or in specially constructed ovens; by 3000 B.C. he was molding these baked bricks into wedge shapes, which he used to line wells and to construct man's first crude arches. It was the third craftsman in clay, however, who most benefited mankind. Scratching symbols onto his wet tablets, he preserved the records, laws and stories that made his own civilization so durable —and helped transmit much of that civilization not only to Mesopotamia's neighbors but also to generations far distant in place and time.

A SNARLING LION'S HEAD *is part of a frieze of glazed brickwork taken from a wall in Babylon.*

# A CITY'S MASSIVE SPLENDOR

On a March day in 1899, a German archeologist named Robert Koldewey began excavating a cluster of mounds on the Euphrates River some 50 miles south of Baghdad. Working for more than a decade, he uncovered the 2,500-year-old ruins of King Nebuchadrezzar's Babylon, the mightiest city of antiquity.

In its heyday, Babylon's wealth and power had no equal in Mesopotamia. So impressive were its architectural splendors—imposing temples, soaring towers and walls decorated with enameled brick *(above)*—that the Greek historian Herodotus wrote in the Fifth Century B.C., "In magnificence, there is no other city that approaches it." For centuries the ruins of this magnificence lay hidden under the desert, but today, working from the findings of archeologists, scholars and artists are able to reconstruct most of the city's finest buildings as they once stood.

*Paintings by Gamal El-Zoghby*

# BABYLON'S MIGHTY WALLS

Koldewey's first discovery at Babylon was debris from a series of massive walls—seen reconstructed in the painting below—that enclosed the inner city of temples and palaces, completed by Nebuchadrezzar in the Sixth Century B.C.

In ancient times these walls, built over the ages by succes-

sive kings, were Babylon's main security against attack. Buttressed at regular intervals by defensive towers, they were so broad across the top, according to Herodotus, that there was "room for a four-horse chariot to turn." The westernmost wall *(right)* rose directly out of the Euphrates, not only providing a defense against invading armies, but also forming a colossal breakwater that protected the city from floods. Above the wall soared the Tower of Babylon, or Babel, the subject of the Bible's tale. Below it, one of the world's oldest masonry bridges, 400 feet long, gave access to the river's opposite bank.

# A GATEWAY
# OF THE GODS

The only structure even partially standing at the time of the excavations at Babylon was an immense ceremonial gateway *(left)*, which guarded the main entrance to the city. It was built so solidly that it survived the destruction of the city by the Persians in the Sixth Century B.C., and subsequent centuries of weathering that leveled most of the surrounding walls.

The gate, dedicated to the goddess Ishtar, consisted of two portals, one behind the other, each flanked by massive towers. Built of kiln-baked bricks cemented with pitch, it was originally covered by a rock-hard outer shell of enameled brick, embellished with brilliantly colored figures of bulls and dragons.

Leading up to the gate was a broad and equally imposing avenue, often used for processions in honor of the god Marduk. Nearly 80 feet wide and paved with slabs of limestone and pink marble, it ran between two walls decorated with an enameled frieze of lions. The avenue's design had a defensive as well as a religious purpose: hemmed in by fortifications, it provided a strategic cul-de-sac where enemy troops storming the Ishtar Gate could be trapped and killed by a shower of arrows shot from the surrounding battlements.

# AN ARCHITECTURE TO DEFY THE SUN

Like the massive city walls that encircled them, the buildings of Babylon were constructed as solidly as fortresses. But, in their case, the main enemy was the oppressive temperatures of the Babylonian summer, which sometimes rose as high as 130 degrees. As insulation against this heat, the ornate façade fronting Nebuchadrezzar's throne room (*above*) was built 10 feet thick, and its three arched entrances faced in a northerly direction so that direct sunlight rarely penetrated the whitewashed interior. The outside walls of private houses (*right*) were virtually windowless, though small courtyards let a dim light into the interior apartments.

NEBUCHADREZZAR'S THRONE ROOM, *faced with a creamy white plaster and colorful friezes of enameled brick, fronted on a broad paved courtyard.*

A PATRICIAN'S DWELLING, *crowded in among other houses in a residential area, was built with a zigzagged façade that broke up its stark exterior.*

# A TOWER
# TO RIVAL HEAVEN

Sheer size made the Tower of Babel the greatest architectural wonder of the ancient world. A huge, many-leveled pyramid surmounted by a temple dedicated to the god Marduk, it soared 300 feet above the surrounding countryside. Its base, 300 feet on a side, rested on a courtyard a quarter of a mile square, enclosed by storehouses and apartments for priests.

The original Tower of Babel, referred to in the Book of Genesis as the epitome of human vanity, was built hundreds of years before the reign of Nebuchadrezzar. Over the centuries it was destroyed, rebuilt and destroyed again. Its last restoration, begun by Nabopolassar, was finished by his son, Nebuchadrezzar himself, who told the royal architects "to raise the top of the Tower that it might rival heaven."

Even after Babylon was devastated by the Persians, the tower continued to haunt the imaginations of men. Alexander the Great, who occupied the ruined city in 331 B.C., planned to rebuild it as a monument to his conquest, but estimated that it would take 10,000 men two months just to clear away its tumbled-down debris. The task proved too great, and the huge edifice was left to crumble through the ages until the modern excavations were begun.

# 8

# MESOPOTAMIA'S RADIANT LIGHT

Civilization is a many-splendored word that to some people means big cities and technological progress, to others, lofty moral and ethical ideas and major achievements in the arts. By any of these criteria, Mesopotamia was the birthplace of civilization, for it was the first place in which man created and sustained—for more than 3,000 years—an urban, literate, technologically sophisticated society, one whose people shared common values and a common view of the origins and order of the world.

Why this should be so—why Mesopotamia, of all places, should have played a key role in generating man's upward climb from barbarism—is not readily apparent. Certainly it was not a promising land for the beginnings of civilized life. Hot, parched and windswept, without wood, stone or minerals, it was not a land likely to lead and influence the world. What turned Mesopotamia into a fruitful paradise and made it a creative force was the intellectual endowment and psychological make-up of its people. Observant, reflective and pragmatic, they tended to grasp what was fundamental and exploit what was possible. Unlike virtually all other ancient peoples, the Mesopotamians evolved a way of life guided by a sense of moderation and balance. Materially and spiritually—in religion and ethics, in politics and economics—they struck a viable mean between reason and fancy, freedom and authority, the knowable and the mysterious.

Equally important, Mesopotamia was an "open" society. Although its inhabitants thought of themselves as a "chosen people," they were by no means provincial. They realized that there were many other peoples in the world, and did not shut themselves off from outside contacts. Thus, while Mesopotamians despised those neighbors who were their enemies, they looked with favor on such peoples as the Egyptians to the west, and the Indus Valley folk to the east. In fact, Mesopotamia may well have played an important role in the rise of both these civilizations.

In the case of Egypt, Mesopotamian influence is apparent in the use of cylinder seals, and in certain motifs in Egyptian art. It is apparent in Egyptian architecture, some of which is constructed of bricks of a size and shape peculiar to early Mesopotamia, and is ornamented with buttresses like

AN ENDURING SYMBOL, *the Tower of Babel represents to this day the vanity of man's ambitions. Originally a tiered temple of Babylon, the tower is seen here in a fanciful illustration from a 15th Century French manuscript.*

those of Sumer. Egypt may also have gotten the idea of writing from its eastern neighbor, even though the hieroglyphs of one and the pictographs of the other are quite different.

Far to the east, the Indus Valley culture, one of archeology's newest finds, apparently had strong commercial ties with Sumer—a number of Indus-type seals have turned up in Mesopotamian ruins. The Indus people inhabited an area larger than Mesopotamia and Egypt combined, and flourished between about 2500 and 1500 B.C. Theirs, too, was an urban culture. Advancing from farming and cattle-breeding, these people became craftsmen and artisans, merchants and administrators. Their houses were built of fine bricks whose uniform dimensions bespeak a standard system of weights and measures. More important, they were a people with a written language, a pictographic script consisting of some 400 characters. Since the two cultures were similar in these respects, and knew each other, it seems logical to suppose that the older culture of Sumer influenced the younger culture of the Indus Valley.

Between India and Mesopotamia lay another land whose debt to Mesopotamian culture is easier to trace. Iran, or Persia, bordered on Mesopotamia and was naturally in intimate contact with it. According to one Sumerian story, the Iranian city-state of Aratta had a political organization and religious beliefs almost identical with those of Sumer. Similarly, the ancient Iranian kingdom of Elam, despite constant and bitter warfare between it and Sumer, was nevertheless deeply influenced by its neighbor. The art and architecture of the Elamites, as well as their law, literature and religion, were Mesopotamian in many of their details —one of Elam's leading deities even had a Sumerian name. The Elamites also adopted Mesopotamia's cuneiform script, as well as its system of education and much of its educational curriculum.

But Mesopotamia's influence upon its contemporaries in Egypt, Iran and India, however inspiring, did not endure. Curiously, its seed took deepest root not among its neighbors, but in the West. Western man's positive, pragmatic, rational outlook found a congenial spirit in the Mesopotamian view of the world. Transfigured by the monotheistic Hebrews, transmuted by the philosophical Greeks, Mesopotamian concepts penetrated the Western ethos, and are responsible in no small part for Western man's turbulent history of tension between reason and faith, hope and despair, freedom and authoritarianism, progress and defeat.

The impact of Mesopotamia on the Hebrews was both direct and circuitous. If, as some scholars think, the Biblical saga of Abraham had a kernel of truth in it, and if the Hebrew patriarch lived in Ur in the days of Hammurabi, then he and his family may have assimilated Sumerian culture long before the Jews themselves were a nation. The Hebrews' ancestors seem clearly to have lived in Mesopotamia from very early times.

Cuneiform documents ranging in date from as early as 1700 down to about 1300 B.C. frequently mention a people called the Habiru, a name closely identified with the Biblical word "Hebrew." According to these texts, the Hebrews were wanderers, nomads, even brigands and outlaws—men who sold their services as mercenaries to Babylonians and Assyrians, Hittites and Hurrians alike. As early as 1500 B.C., these archetypal ancestors of the Wandering Jew began the conquest of Palestine. There they came in contact with the Canaanites, a people who had borrowed richly from Mesopotamia. The Canaanites had a cuneiform script, their schools followed the Mesopotamian curriculum and their culture was deeply imbued with Mesopotamian thought and belief.

The Hebrews' most important contact with Mesopotamian culture began in 586 B.C., when King

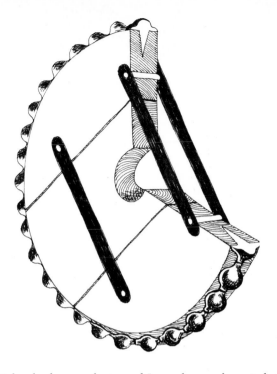

AN ARCHETYPAL WHEEL, *shown in a schematic drawing based on wheels from Susa and Kish, consisted of three rounded pieces of wood held together by metal ties and rimmed with copper studs.*

Nebuchadrezzar destroyed Jerusalem and carried off its people into Babylonian captivity. The literacy and great learning of the Babylonians infiltrated the Hebrew mind and Hebrew thought. When the exiles later returned to their homeland to create the Judean state, they carried with them a number of Mesopotamia's liturgical, educational and legal practices. Some of these carried over into Christianity and, via the Judeo-Christian tradition, reached Western civilization as a whole.

The second people who absorbed Mesopotamian culture and funneled it westward were the Greeks. Unlike the Hebrews, they had no direct contact with Mesopotamia itself, but, during Greece's Mycenaean Age, from about 1600 to 1100 B.C., they did have close political and commercial ties with Mesopotamia's neighbors, the Hittites and Canaanites. Through the coastal towns of southern Anatolia, Canaan, Cyprus and Crete flowed not only material goods, but thoughts and ideas—undoubtedly to take root on Greek soil. The discovery in Greek Thebes only a few years ago of an impressive cache of Babylonian cylinder seals was not altogether surprising to the archeological world, and the future will no doubt reveal numerous such finds on Greek soil.

This early contact with the Near East came to an end when the Mycenaean culture collapsed. Not until the Eighth Century B.C., when the Greeks began to emerge from their "Dark Age," were they once again stimulated and inspired by their eastern neighbors. During this later period, the Canaanite Phoenicians gave the Greeks the alphabet that eventually became the alphabet of the entire Western world. During this period, too, pre-Socratic Greek philosophers in Anatolia discovered the works of Babylonian astronomers and began the cosmological studies that culminated in the great philosophical schools of Athens. By the time Greece entered its Golden Age, in the Fifth Century B.C., not a few of its achievements in art, architecture, philosophy and literature showed vestiges of Mesopotamian origin.

Moving westward through the channels of Hellenism, Judaism and Christianity, Mesopotamia's legacy to mankind eventually reached the modern world. In technology, that legacy included such prosaic miracles as the wheeled vehicle and the seeder-plow. In science, it included the beginnings of astronomy and a numerical system based on 60 —a system still in use today, dividing the circle into degrees and the hour into minutes and seconds. Mesopotamia's astronomical observations led to the eventual discovery of the seasonal equinoxes and the regularity of the phases of the moon. And astronomy's pseudo-scientific adjunct, astrology, revealed through its interpretations of the "writing of heaven" the fixed relationships of the stars. It was Mesopotamia that invented zodiacal names— the Bull, the Twins, the Lion, the Scorpion and many others.

Mesopotamia also gave Western civilization two of its most important political institutions—the city-state and the concept of a divinely sanctioned kingship. The city-state spread over much of the Mediterranean world, and kingship—the notion that a ruler's right to rule was bestowed by the gods, and that he was accountable to them for his stewardship—passed into the very fiber of Western society. It is hardly coincidence that British monarchs today go through coronation ceremonies so reminiscent of those of Mesopotamia. Nor can it be a coincidence that activities traditionally associated with monarchs appeared in the early archives of Mesopotamian kings. Through highly efficient government bureaucracies, which used sophisticated bookkeeping and accounting systems, the Mesopotamian rulers administered the building and repairing of roads, the construction of hostelries for travelers, the sailing of the seas for trade and barter, the arbitration of political disputes and the writing of international treaties.

One of Mesopotamia's most precious political legacies was the written law. Originating in an awareness of the rights of the individual—and fostered by a penchant for controversy and litigation —Mesopotamian law evolved into a lofty ideal, conceived to be divinely inspired for the benefit of all society. Words derived from Babylonian and Sumerian legal traditions occur throughout the vast, heterogeneous commentary on Hebrew law known as the Babylonian Talmud. "To this very day," wrote the late E. A. Speiser, a leading authority on ancient legal systems, "the orthodox Jew uses a Sumerian term when he speaks of divorce. And when he participates in the reading of the Torah lesson in the synagogue, he still touches the pertinent place in the scroll with the fringe of his prayer shawl, wholly unaware of the fact that he is thus re-enacting the scene in which the ancient Mesopotamian impressed the hem of his garment on a clay tablet, as proof of his commitment to the provisions of the legal record."

Probably it is no exaggeration to say that Mesopotamian law shed its light over much of the civilized world. Greece and Rome were influenced by it through their contacts with the Near East, and Islam acquired a formal legal code only after it had conquered the region that is now Iraq, the homeland of ancient Mesopotamia. Just how much of modern law goes back to Mesopotamian origins has yet to be determined, but the British historian H. W. F. Saggs notes in his book, *The Greatness That Was Babylon*, that "the law dealing with mortgage almost certainly goes back ultimately . . . to the ancient Near East."

Similarly, Mesopotamia's rich complex of ritual and myth, evolved by a remarkable group of theologians who lived 3,000 years before the birth of Christ, profoundly affected the religions of the West—especially Judaism and Christianity. The Mesopotamian notion that water was the source of all creation found its way, for instance, into the Genesis account of the creation of the world, and the Biblical view that man was fashioned of clay and imbued with the "breath of life" goes back to Mesopotamian roots. So, too, does the Biblical concept that man was created primarily to serve God and that God's creative power is in His Word. The idea that catastrophes are divine punishment for wrongdoing, and that pain and suffering must be submitted to patiently, also have striking Mesopotamian parallels. Even the Mesopotamian's netherworld, his dark, dreary "Land of No Return," had its counterpart in the Hebrews' *Sheol* and the Hades of the Greeks.

To this day, Jewish liturgy is replete with Babylonian borrowings. The Kol Nidre, the Jewish chant recited on the eve of the Day of Atonement, asking forgiveness for the breaking of vows, is similar to prayers that were part of the Mesopotamian New Year's ceremonies. So, too, is the solemn description of man's fate that is recited on the Day of Atonement itself. From their Babylonian exile, the Hebrews also acquired a belief in demons and demon-exorcism, which no doubt explains several New Testament passages concerned with the casting out of devils.

From the days of the Babylonian captivity on,

Judaism swarmed with religious mystics who had apocalyptic visions about the future of man. Through these visionaries, says the eminent Oriéntalist W. F. Albright, "innumerable elements of pagan imagery and even entire myths entered into the literature of Judaism and Christianity." The rite of Baptism, for instance, he says, goes back to the religions of Mesopotamia, and so do many of the elements in the story of the life of Christ. Among these, Dr. Albright includes the virgin birth, its association with the stars and the themes of imprisonment, death, descent to the underworld, disappearance for three days, and eventual ascension to heaven.

Mesopotamian religion was, of course, pagan and polytheistic, and is therefore separated by a profound spiritual gulf from the monotheism of Judaism and Christianity. Moreover, both the Old and New Testaments are imbued with an ethical sensitivity and moral fervor that have no counterparts in the comparable Mesopotamian documents. Neither Sumer, nor Babylon, nor Assyria ever arrived at the lofty persuasion that a "pure heart" and "clean hands" were spiritually more meaningful than elaborate rituals and sacrifices. The bond of love between god and man, while not entirely absent from Mesopotamian religious thought, is certainly far less significant there than it is in Judaism and Christianity. But the early Mesopotamians did develop the concept of a personal and family god, echoed in the Biblical "god of Abraham, Isaac and Jacob"—and between this guardian deity and his adoring worshiper there was a tender, close and trusting relationship comparable in some ways to the one that existed between Jehovah and the patriarchs.

Mesopotamian literature, like its religion and law, has also affected the entire Western world. Themes in the initial chapters of Genesis—the Creation, Paradise, the Flood, the Cain-Abel rivalry, the Babel of Tongues—all have Mesopotamian literary antecedents. Many a psalm in the Book of Psalms is reminiscent of Mesopotamian cultic hymns, and the Book of Lamentations copies a favorite literary device of Mesopotamian writers—in Sumer it was common to compose formal lamentations for the destruction of a city. There are also stylistic antecedents for the Book of Proverbs in Sumerian collections of sayings, maxims and adages. Even the Song of Solomon, a book unlike any of the others in the Old Testament, may have had an earlier Mesopotamian counterpart in the Sumerian cultic love song.

Greek literature, too, shows innumerable traces of Mesopotamian influence. The Mesopotamian flood story, for example, is paralleled in Greek mythology by the story of Deucalion, who builds a boat and in it survives a deluge that destroys the rest of mankind. The dragon-slaying theme in

Mesopotamian myths has its counterparts in such Greek tales as those of Jason and Heracles, both of whom killed several monsters. Plagues sent as punishment by the gods also figure in the mythology of Greece and Mesopotamia. And there is a marked resemblance between the Greek and Mesopotamian netherworlds, both of which were gloomy places separated from the realm of the living by an ominous river across which the dead were ferried. Similarly, the Greek dirge, or elegy for the dead, seems to have a forerunner in two Sumerian compositions, recently translated from a tablet in Moscow's Pushkin Museum; in them a Mesopotamian poet bemoans in hyperbolic language the death of his father and his wife. Even the form of the Greek epic, the medium that produced the *Iliad* and the *Odyssey*, had its counterpart in the style of Mesopotamian epics.

In the area of Greek "wisdom" literature, scholars have also lately uncovered a number of Mesopotamian parallels. Several of Aesop's fables have Sumerian predecessors, and the instructions in an 18th Century B.C. version of a Sumerian farmer's almanac are strangely like those in *Works and Days*, a farmer's manual composed some 10 centuries later by the Greek poet Hesiod. A number of Sumerian dialogues are now being pieced together and deciphered, and these, too, may turn out to be stylistic precursors of such masterpieces as Plato's *Dialogues*.

In another field, music and musical theory, the Mesopotamian contribution has only just been discovered. Archeologists have known for many years that Mesopotamia had musical instruments, particularly harps and lyres. Sir Leonard Woolley, for example, in his excavations at Ur, uncovered the remains of nine lyres and two harps. And a hymn dedicated to King Shulgi of Ur boasts that the king knows how to play the "sweet three-necked lyre, . . . [a] heart-expanding three-stringed instrument,"

and some 10 other musical instruments not identified. Musicians were trained in schools and formed an important professional class in Mesopotamia, some becoming high court officials. But no one knew anything about the music itself until recently, when Anne Darffkorn Kilner of the University of California at Berkeley, a cuneiformist, and Madame Duchesne-Guillemin of the University of Liège, Belgium, a musicologist, teamed up to interpret the contents of a cuneiform tablet that had mystified scholars for 70 years.

The main clue to the tablet's contents was a series of numbers apparently referring to the strings of a nine-stringed instrument. Once this was established, it was found that the numbers were arranged in a progression that suggested the tuning of this instrument, and that other notations described what appeared to be the intervals in a musical scale. The inscriptions on this clay tablet, which probably dates from about 1500 B.C., carry the history of music and musical theory back to more than a millennium before the first-known Greek musical notations. It is, in fact, the first record in history of a musical scale and a coherent musical system.

The wide evidence of Mesopotamia's contributions to civilization in all fields is still only a small fraction of the total—the visible portion of the iceberg. It is no easy task to trace ideas and techniques, themes and motifs down through the ages to their place of origin; the threads of transmission are gossamer-fine and often elude the searching eye and mind. Future discoveries will undoubtedly add new facets to the picture, and just as surely bring many surprises. But the future can only confirm what is already apparent—that Mesopotamia, with its unique combination of geography and human genius, created a culture without precedent: the land between the Tigris and Euphrates Rivers will always be considered the Cradle of Civilization.

A SUMERIAN MASTERWORK, *this elegant marble head set a standard of artistic merit still respected today.*

# PILLARS OF CIVILIZATION

Down through the millennia, Mesopotamia still speaks to the world. This land, made productive through irrigation, allowed man for the first time to rise above the level of mere subsistence, giving him the time to think and the resources to develop creatively. From the blossoming of ideas, institutions and techniques that resulted have come major tools of civilization, since altered in detail but never in basic concept. It was in Sumer that systems of trade and a merchant class evolved. It was there too that the first practical system of writing developed, initially so that business accounts could be kept. It was the Sumerians who devised the first wheeled vehicle, the written code of law, the bicameral legislature and government by elected rulers. And a Sumerian poem first alluded to a golden age that still haunts the dreams of man: "Once upon a time there was no snake, there was no scorpion . . . There was no fear, no terror. Man had no rival . . ."

CUNEIFORM ACCOUNTING TABLET, 1980 B.C.

HEBREW BIBLICAL TEXT, 20TH CENTURY

CHECK NUMERALS AND SYMBOLS FOR COMPUTERIZED ACCOUNTING, 1967

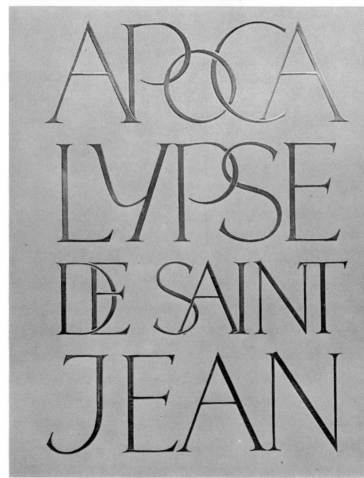

MODERN HAND LETTERING, FRENCH BIBLICAL TEXT, 1961

# THE WRITTEN WORD

More than any other human invention, writing made civilization possible. As pictographs gave way to Sumerian cuneiform *(above)* and this in turn yielded to the alphabetical writing of the Phoenicians, man gained step-by-step an expanding power to accumulate and transmit the knowledge of the past. Society acquired a history and systematic human learning became possible. Until the 15th Century, writing remained a skill of the minority, kept alive during medieval days largely by monks who painstakingly handlettered illuminated manuscripts *(far right)*. But after 1440 the invention of printing made it possible to publish written works. With printing came mass literacy and an explosion of the written word; by 1900 newspapers were being turned out at a million copies a day. In the 1960s, even as 400,000 new publications were appearing annually, a new kind of printing *(center)*, legible to the electronic eyes of computers, was enabling modern man to record and use more knowledge than the Sumerian scribes could have dreamed.

EGYPTIAN HIEROGLYPHICS, EARLY 2ND MILLENNIUM B.C.

Maum confolator orbif interpretatur inere par euutarem fanguinum et poft euerfi onem illiuf loquitur Ecce super montes pedef euangelizantif et annunciantif pacem.

INCIPIT NAVM PROPHETA

HANDWRITTEN LATIN BIBLE, ITALY, 1478

JEAN

AUX SEPT ÉGLISES D'ASIE.

GRACE ET PAIX VOUS SOIENT DONNÉES PAR "Il est, Il était et Il vient", par les sept Esprits présents devant son trône, 5 et par Jésus Christ, le témoin fidèle, le premier-né d'entre les morts, le Prince des rois de la terre. Il nous aime et nous a lavés de nos péchés par son sang, 6 Il a fait de

7

CART WITH EARLY SPOKED WHEELS, GREEK VASE DECORATION, 550 B.C.

CHARIOT MODEL, EARLY SUMERIAN

# THE WHEEL

In the Fourth Millennium B.C., some Sumerian craftsman built the first known wheeled vehicle, probably much like the small model above, made as a burial offering. With wheels on axles, one ox could now haul two to three times as much weight as before. The Sumerians' solid wooden wheel, the greatest mechanical invention of all time, remained essentially unchanged for centuries. Some 1,900 years later, lighter, spoked wheels carried Egyptian charioteers into battle *(top center)* and by the Middle Ages wheels on swiveling front axles made carts steerable *(right)*. Wheeled vehicles could now move faster, but not fast or cheaply enough to satisfy the demands of the Industrial Revolution. The answer, which came in 1804, was the steam-propelled, iron-wheeled locomotive, which soon moved loads 15 times faster than the horse-drawn wagon. Mass movements of goods and people were assured, but the wheel's biggest turn was to come in the 20th Century. Then, rubber-tired and gasoline-driven, it brought the age of the automobile.

MEDIEVAL CART, FRENCH, 13TH CENTURY

...RIOT, EGYPTIAN, 2ND MILLENNIUM B.C.

MODEL T FORD, 1908

...Y CARRIAGE, U.S., LATE 19TH CENTURY

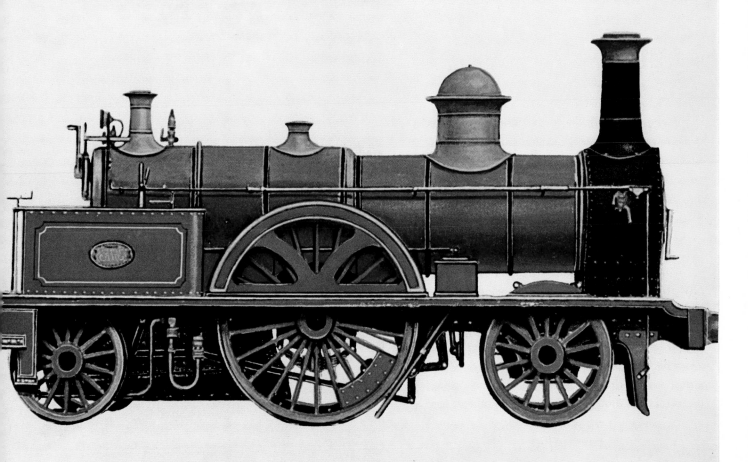

...RESS LOCOMOTIVE, ENGLAND, 1861

HEADDRESS OF QUEEN SHUDU-AD, SUMER, THIRD MILLENNIUM, B.C.

MASK OF AN ACHAEAN KING, MYCENAE, 16TH CENTURY B.C.

# THE CONCEPT OF KINGS

At first the rulers of Sumer were outstanding commoners elected to lead their people during crises, but soon these democratically chosen chieftains were transformed into hereditary monarchs who ruled with divine sanction, setting the pattern for centuries to come. Some of their successors, like Greece's Alexander the Great and Persia's Shapur II, actually considered themselves to be gods; others, like the legendary King Arthur, thought merely to be vicars of the Lord; France's absolutist Louis XIV saw kings "occupying, so to speak, the place of God." Yet even "absolute" monarchs had to observe the unwritten laws of their lands. England's Elizabeth I did, most cannily, and won her people; Charles I did not, and lost his head. With the rise of democracy, monarchies that could not adapt declined; in 1945 Europe counted only ten kings. And with democracies, once more, came rulers chosen not because of royal bloodlines but because of merit, elected for specific duties of leadership, and for limited periods of time.

HEAD OF A PERSIAN KING (THOUGHT TO BE SHAPUR II), FOURTH CENTURY A.D.

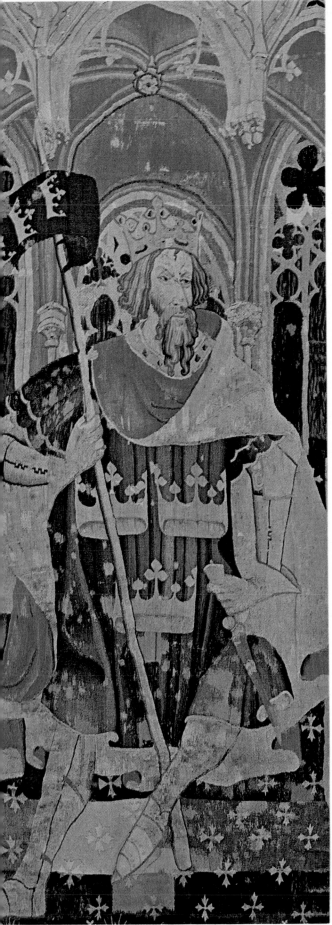

KING ARTHUR, 14TH CENTURY FRENCH TAPESTRY

QUEEN ELIZABETH I OF ENGLAND, PAINTING BY GUILLEM STRETES, 1559

KING LOUIS XIV OF FRANCE, PAINTING BY HYACINTHE RIGAUD, 1701

HAMMURABI RECEIVING HIS CODE FROM A GOD, STELE, 18TH CENTURY B.C.

THE SCALES OF JUSTICE, FROM A FRESCO BY LORENZETTI, 1338-1339

# A SOCIETY OF LAWS

A shaft of black diorite, unearthed in 1901, is the first great monument to man's continuing search for justice. It records the code of Babylon's King Hammurabi *(above)*—a list of crimes and penalties demanding, in essence, an eye for an eye and a tooth for a tooth. Five centuries later, the Mosaic Code *(right)* still echoed this harsh doctrine. But by the Sixth Century A.D. Justinian's Code was shifting the emphasis from punishment to due process, ruling that a man was innocent until proved guilty. In 1215, England's nobles forced King John to sign the Magna Carta, which recognized such basic rights as that to a fair trial. Over the centuries the law continued to grow, adapting to the changing needs of society as it progressed, from the Napoleonic Code of 1804, which legalized the reforms of the French Revolution, to the civil rights decisions of today's U.S. Supreme Court. The search for justice still goes on, attempting to fulfill the promise made by Hammurabi 4,000 years ago: "The oppressed . . . shall read the writing . . . and he shall find his right."

MOSES WITH THE TABLETS OF LAW, PAINTING BY REMBRANDT, 1659

THE LAWYERS, PAINTING BY HONORÉ DAUMIER, 1854-1856

# CROSSROAD
# CIVILIZATIONS BETWEEN
# EAST AND WEST

The chart at right is designed to show the duration of ancient Mesopotamian civilization, and to relate it to others in the "Crossroad" group of cultures that are considered in one major group of volumes in this series. This chart is excerpted from a comprehensive world chronology that appears in the introductory booklet of the series. Comparison of the chart with the world chronology will enable the reader to relate early Mesopotamian culture to important cultural periods in other parts of the world.

On the following pages is a chronological listing of important events that took place in the period covered by this book.

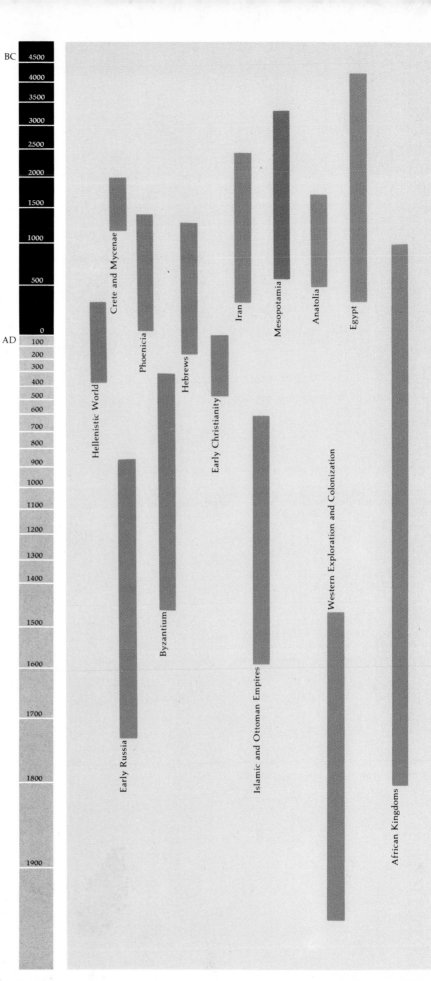

# CHRONOLOGY: *A listing of significant events in ancient Mesopotamia*

| B.C. | Period | Culture | History |
|---|---|---|---|
| 9000 | | The people of Karim Shahir, a small campsite in the Zagros foothills, begin to cultivate wild wheat and barley and domesticate dogs and sheep, inaugurating the change from a food-gathering to a food-producing society | |
| 7000 | EARLY FARMING COMMUNITIES | At Jarmo, in the Zagros foothills, one of the oldest known permanent settlements, the inhabitants build crude mud houses, grow wheat from seed, and herd goats, sheep and pigs | |
| 5000 | | The Hassuna culture introduces irrigation, fine pottery and permanent dwellings — The Halafan culture dominates Mesopotamia for 1,000 years and develops trade from the Persian Gulf to the Mediterranean | Northern farmers migrate southward and settle in the region stretching from Babylon to the Persian Gulf |
| 4500 | PRE-SUMERIANS | Division of labor first appears among the Ubaidians, who build villages of mud brick, construct religious shrines and exert a civilizing force in the south for 1,000 years | |
| 4000 | | A small temple at Eridu contains the earliest example of an offering table and a niche for a cult object | Semitic nomads from Syria and the Arabian peninsula invade southern Mesopotamian territory and intermingle with the Ubaidian population |
| 3500 | | Cylinder seals are used to identify ownership of documents and vessels — The Northern Temple at Tepe Gawra is built with buttressed walls, setting the style for later temples — A temple at Eridu, earliest prototype of the ziggurat, is built on a small terrace | Sumerians settle on the banks of the Euphrates, probably after migrating from Central Asia through Iran |
| 3000 | | Sumerians introduce pictographs, an early form of writing, to keep administrative records — Sculptors begin making three-dimensional statues, such as the Warka head — The traditional design of the ziggurat appears in the White Temple, which includes an approaching stairway — Colored mosaics begin to be used as decoration for buildings, such as the Painted Temple at Tell Uqair | Democratic assemblies give way to kingships of limited authority, which evolve into hereditary monarchies — Kish becomes the leading Sumerian city during the reign of Etana — Meskiaggasher founds Sumerian Erech's first dynasty, rivaling Kish |
| 2750 | SUMERIANS | The first formal contracts for land sales are drawn up, written in cuneiform — Small, simple palaces are built at the Sumerian cities of Eridu and Kish — "Praying statues," from Eshnunna (Tell Asmar), indicate the use of expressionistic techniques to show religious feeling | |
| 2500 | | The "Standard of Ur," an inlaid plaque commemorating war and peace, religious statues, and many gold and silver artifacts are buried in the tombs of Ur — The "Stele of the Vultures," an outstanding example of Sumerian bas-relief, marks the victory of King Eannatum over the city of Umma — Sargon builds his magnificent Akkadian capital of Agade | Gilgamesh, hero of Sumerian legends, reigns as king of Erech — Brief rule of Sumer by Elamites of Iran is ended by King Lugalannemundu of Adab, who unites the Sumerian city-states — Sumerian city-states vie for domination over a period of 200 years — King Eannatum raises the city-state of Lagash to a pinnacle of power through military conquests — King Lugalzaggesi of Umma overthrows the hegemony of Lagash — Sargon the Great of Akkad conquers Lugalzaggesi to take control of Umma |
| 2250 | | Gudea, Prince of Lagash, becomes a patron of art and literature, and magnificent statues are produced in his honor — Ur-Nammu dedicates a ziggurat at Ur to the moon-god Nanna and also sets up an early | Naram-Sin, grandson of Sargon, extends Akkadian dominance into Armenia and Iran — Gutians from Iran conquer Sumer and destroy Agade — Lagash, under Prince Gudea, prospers despite Gutian domination — Utuhegal, King of Erech, overthrows the Gutians — Ur-Nammu founds Ur's third Sumerian dynasty |

## BABYLONIANS AND ASSYRIANS

| Date (B.C.) | Events |
|---|---|
| 2000 | With the fall of Ur, Mesopotamian art and architecture decline in creativity and spontaneity |
| 2000 | Elamites attack and destroy Ur |
| 1900 | Amorites from Syrian Desert conquer Sumer |
| 1900 | The Amorite sheikh Sumuabum founds first dynasty in Babylon |
| 1800 | Hammurabi ascends the throne of Babylon |
| 1800 | King Zimrilim of Mari, in Syria, becomes one of Hammurabi's chief adversaries |
| 1800 | Hammurabi brings most of Mesopotamia under his control |
| 1700 | Hammurabi introduces his Law Code |
| 1600 | The end of Hammurabi's dynasty is marked by Hittite invasions from Turkey |
| 1600 | Exploiting the destruction inflicted by the Hittites, Kassites from the Zagros Mountains assume control of Babylonia for the next four centuries |
| 1500 | Assyria is conquered by Hurrians from Anatolia |
| 1400 | Bas-relief of baked brick appears as a dominant art form in the Karaindash Temple in Erech |
| 1400 | Assuruballit regains Assyrian independence after decline of Hurrian power |
| 1400 | King Kurigalzu assumes the Babylonian throne |
| 1300 | King Kurigalzu of Babylon builds the fortified city of Dur-Kurigalzu, dominated by a lofty ziggurat |
| 1200 | Nebuchadrezzar I expels the Elamites from Babylonia |
| 1200 | Babylonians invade Assyria but are routed before reaching Assur, the capital |
| 1100 | Iron, introduced originally by the Hittites, is used extensively in Assyria for tools and weapons |
| 1100 | King Tiglath-Pileser I leads Assyria to a new era of power, expands his influence into Asia Minor and exacts tribute from Mediterranean coastal cities |
| 1100 | After Tiglath-Pileser's death, Aramaean tribes and Zagros mountaineers rise and shatter the Assyrian empire |
| 1000 | Adadnirari II leads Assyria out of a century and a half of decline to a position of power |
| 900 | Assyria's Assurnasirpal II, grandson of Adadnirari, builds a magnificent new capital, Calah (present-day Nimrud), replacing the old capital of Assur |
| 900 | Assyrian bas-reliefs turn from religious themes to glorification of kings |
| 900 | Shalmaneser III ascends the Assyrian throne as a successor to his father Assurnasirpal II and conquers areas rich in iron and timber |
| 800 | Sargon II of Assyria begins the 10-year task of building a new capital at Dur-Sharrukin |
| 800 | Tiglath-Pileser III comes to the Assyrian throne and creates a great empire extending from the Persian Gulf to the borders of Egypt |
| 800 | Sargon II is enthroned in Assyria and subdues an empire in revolt |
| 800 | Sargon's son, Sennacherib, destroys Babylon |
| 700 | Sennacherib's son, Esarhaddon, rebuilds Babylon |
| 700 | King Assurbanipal assumes the rule of Assyria, governing an empire that extends from the Nile to the Caucasus Mountains |
| 700 | Chaldeans and Iranian Medes overrun Assyria, destroying Nineveh and Assur and ushering in the Neo-Babylonian empire |
| 600 | Nebuchadrezzar II of Babylon builds the "Tower of Babel" and a temple to Marduk |
| 600 | Babylon's last king, Nabonidus, rebuilds the Ur-Nammu ziggurat |
| 600 | Nebuchadrezzar II rules the Neo-Babylonian empire |
| 600 | Nebuchadrezzar II razes Jerusalem and takes the Jews into captivity in Babylon |
| 500 | Cyrus the Great, Persia's brilliant warrior and statesman, conquers Babylon |

## HOW THE ARCHEOLOGIST DATES

**FIRST DYNASTY OF UR**
2400-3000 B.C.
*Building levels*

**1**

O ft. *Ground level*

23 ft.

**JEMDET NASR-UBAID III**
3000-4500 B.C.

*Ashes with kiln remains
and quantities of shards*

*Jemdet Nasr ware
3000-3200 B.C.*

*Erech ware
3200-3800 B.C.*

*Ubaidian ware
3800-4500 B.C.*

41 ft.

*Sand deposited by flood*

52 ft.

*Refuse and remains
of crude dwellings*

57 ft.

**UBAID I**
4500-4900 B.C.
*Mud with scattering
of shards*

60 ft.

*Virgin soil:
packed clay and marsh reeds*

**1** STRATIGRAPHY, the study of the levels of a site, is the most basic and important archeological technique for piecing together history. It exposes the sequence of successive human settlements, built one over another, from the oldest layers of remains at the bottom to the most recent layers at the top.

Archeologists excavating the city of Ur in southern Mesopotamia, for instance, dug a shaft some 60 feet down, reaching soil undisturbed by human activity and exposing above it a section (*chart, left*) that represented some 25 centuries of civilization. On the lowest level of habitation they found remains of reed huts, dwellings of a prehistoric people known as the Ubaidians. Above this level was a band 11 feet deep of sand, deposited by a huge overflowing of the Tigris and Euphrates, a catastrophe apparently recalled in the Biblical story of the Flood. Only a few of the Ubaidians seem to have survived the deluge, and they were eventually succeeded by two other cultures. Above the artifacts of all these peoples lay the ruined houses, temples and tombs of the Sumerians.

The shaft at Ur, like all stratigraphical evidence, provides scholars with an accurate sequence of events. To obtain a definite date for each stratum, however, archeologists must study the findings embedded in it. Two methods for doing this are described on the opposite page.

**3**

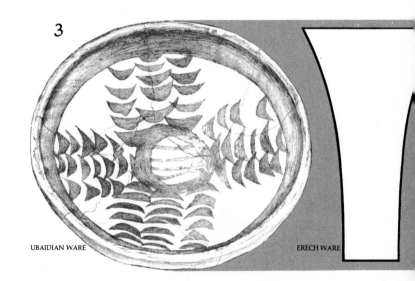

UBAIDIAN WARE

ERECH WARE

# SITES AND FINDINGS

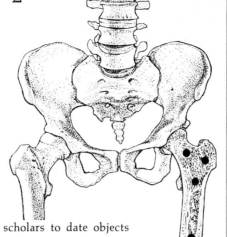

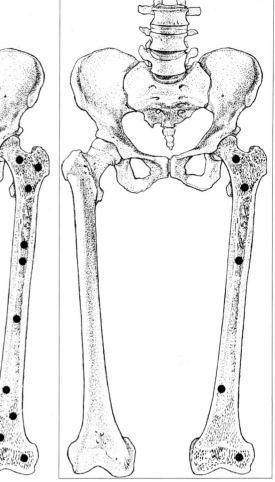

**2** CARBON 14 DATING permits scholars to date objects from cultures that have left no written records. This technique is based on the fact that all living organisms, both plant and animal, absorb radioactivity while they are alive and surrender it after they are dead. The rate at which dead organisms give up their radioactivity is fixed. Thus, while he was alive, the bones of a prehistoric human being contained a known number of radioactive carbon 14 atoms, symbolized by the black dots in the skeleton at near right. But, as the skeleton at far right shows, half of these atoms have lost their radioactivity 5,600 years after the man's death. By counting the surviving atoms, scientists can determine when any organism died. In Mesopotamia the technique has provided dates for the earliest agricultural villages, and also for such important figures as Hammurabi, the Babylonian ruler and lawgiver.

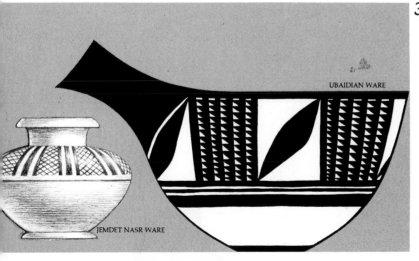

UBAIDIAN WARE

JEMDET NASR WARE

**3** AN ANALYSIS OF POTTERY has helped archeologists deduce the history of Mesopotamia. At Ur, a pottery factory was in continuous operation for more than 1,000 years, and the shaft dug at the site went through a yard where potters discarded imperfect ware. These shards, thrown away over the centuries, represented three different styles of pottery, shown in the sketch at left.

The kind found just above the flood level was Ubaidian ware. This pottery was hand-turned and decorated with geometric designs. Great quantities of it were unearthed below the flood level, but only a little above; this led archeologists to surmise that too few of the original settlers survived the flood to resist the next people, represented by the next level of pottery. These invaders, the Erech people, made a ware that was generally simple in shape and molded on potters' wheels. The Erech culture in turn gave way to the Jemdet Nasr people, whose well-fired jars appear in the next stratum.

By relating these styles to similar pieces found at other sites, for which dates were already known, archeologists determined that the Ubaidian pottery was made roughly between 4500 and 3800 B.C., the Erech ware between 3800 and 3200 and the Jemdet Nasr pottery between 3200 and 3000. These dates, of course, applied not only to the pottery but also to all the other artifacts in those levels.

# ART INFORMATION AND PICTURE CREDITS

*The sources for the illustrations in "Cradle of Civilization" are set forth below. Descriptive notes on all the works of art are included. Credits for pictures positioned from left to right are separated by semicolons, from top to bottom by dashes. Photographers' names that follow a descriptive note appear in parentheses. Circa is abbreviated "ca."*

COVER—Votive statuettes from Abu Temple at Tell Asmar, gypsum, shell and lapis lazuli, early Third Millennium B.C., Iraq Museum, Baghdad (Dr. Georg Gerster from Rapho Guillumette). 8-9—Map by Leo and Diane Dillon (Ed Isaacs Studio, Inc.).

CHAPTER 1: 10—Female figurine from Nippur, green alabaster and gold, early Third Millennium B.C., Iraq Museum, Baghdad (David Lees). 17-29—Dr. Georg Gerster from Rapho Guillumette.

CHAPTER 2: 30—Head of an Akkadian king, bronze, late Third Millennium B.C., Iraq Museum, Baghdad (Hirmer Fotoarchiv, München). 32-33—Drawings by Shelly Sacks. 37—Drawing by Donald and Ann Crews, after Plate 21 B in Vol. I of *A History of Technology*, Oxford University Press, courtesy of the University Museum, Philadelphia. 38—Map by Rafael D. Palacios. 41-49—"Royal Standard of Ur," front and back sides and details, shell, lapis lazuli and red stone inlaid in wood, early Third Millennium B.C., courtesy of the Trustees of the British Museum, London.

CHAPTER 3: 50—Eagle-headed genius from palace of King Assurnasirpal II at Nimrud, alabaster frieze, early First Millennium B.C., Musée du Louvre, Paris (Hirmer Fotoarchiv, München). 58-59—Maps by Rafael D. Palacios. 63-77—All pictures scenes from palace of King Assurbanipal at Nineveh, alabaster friezes, early First Millennium B.C., courtesy of the Trustees of the British Museum, London. 63-64—Photograph by Hirmer Fotoarchiv, München. 65—Photograph courtesy of the British Museum, London—photograph by Hirmer Fotoarchiv, München. 66-67—Photograph courtesy of the British Museum, London. 68-69—Photograph by Hirmer Fotoarchiv, München—photograph courtesy of the British Museum, London. 70-71—Photograph courtesy of the British Museum, London. 72-77—Photographs by Hirmer Fotoarchiv, München.

CHAPTER 4: 78—Votive figures from Tell Asmar, stone with inlaid shell and lapis lazuli eyes, early Third Millennium B.C., Oriental Institute, Chicago, and Iraq Museum, Baghdad (photograph courtesy of the Oriental Institute, University of Chicago). 81—Drawings by Gamal El-Zoghby after *Excavations at Ur* by Sir Leonard Woolley. 82—Two views of head of a woman wearing turban, limestone, early Third Millennium B.C., Iraq Museum, Baghdad (Hirmer Fotoarchiv, München); two views of statuette of a woman, limestone, early Third Millennium B.C., courtesy of the Trustees of the British Museum, London (Hirmer Fotoarchiv, München); detail of statuette of woman wearing a "polos," gypsum, early Third Millennium B.C., Damascus Museum, Syria (Hirmer Fotoarchiv, München); two views of statue of a goddess, white stone, early Second Millennium B.C., Aleppo Museum, Syria (Hirmer Fotoarchiv, München). 84—Drawing by Shelly Sacks after design by William A. Baker, Curator of the Hart Nautical Museum, Massachusetts Institute of Technology—drawing by Shelly Sacks. 87-97—Photographs by Tor Eigeland from Black Star. 89—Seal impression, late Fourth Millennium B.C., courtesy of the Oriental Institute, University of Chicago. 91—Detail of relief on stone trough, early Third Millennium B.C., courtesy of the Trustees of the British Museum, London. 94—Seal impression, middle Third Millennium B.C., courtesy of the Trustees of the British Museum, London.

CHAPTER 5: 98—Sumerian religious figure, gold, silver, shell, lapis lazuli and red limestone, middle Third Millennium B.C., courtesy of the University Museum, Philadelphia (Lee Boltin). 100-101—Wood carvings by Nicholas Fasciano (Donald Miller). 105—Eye idol from Tell Brak, alabaster, late Fourth Millennium B.C., courtesy of the Trustees of the British Museum, London. 109-117—Illustrations by Leo and Diane Dillon. 118—Seated statue of Gudea, diorite, late Third Millennium B.C., The Metropolitan Museum of Art, Harris Brisbane Dick Fund, 1959 (Norman Snyder). 120—"Major General Sir Henry Creswicke Rawlinson," H. W. Phillips, mezzotint from original portrait, 1850, courtesy Thames and Hudson, Ltd., London. 125—Statuette of Dudu the Scribe, early Third Millennium B.C., gray stone, Iraq Museum, Baghdad (Hirmer Fotoarchiv, München). 129—Scenes from palace of King Tiglath-Pileser III at Nimrud, alabaster relief, middle First Millennium B.C., courtesy of the Trustees of the British Museum, London. 130-131—Bull's head, bronze with inlaid shell

and lapis lazuli eyes, early Fourth Millennium B.C., Musée du Louvre, Paris (Archives Photographiques, Paris)—tablets made and inscribed by Abdul-Hadi A. Al-Fouadi, University of Pennsylvania, Philadelphia (Lee Boltin). 132-133—Tablets made and inscribed by Abdul-Hadi A. Al-Fouadi, University of Pennsylvania, Philadelphia (Lee Boltin). 134—Babylonian World Map tablet, middle First Millennium B.C., courtesy of the Trustees of the British Museum, London—duck weight, black stone, late Third Millennium B.C., Iraq Museum, Baghdad (Hirmer Fotoarchiv, München)—Neo-Babylonian barrel cylinder, middle First Millennium B.C., courtesy of the Trustees of the British Museum, London—inscribed male statue from Mari, breccia, early Third Millennium B.C., Aleppo Museum, Syria (Hirmer Fotoarchiv, München). 135—Accounting tablet, early Third Millennium B.C., Iraq Museum, Baghdad (Frank Scherschel)—Pharmacopoeia tablet, late Third Millennium B.C., courtesy of the University Museum, Philadelphia. 136-137—Photographs by Professor George C. Cameron.

CHAPTER 7: 138—Front panel of sound box of harp, shell inlay and niello, early Third Millennium B.C., University Museum, Philadelphia (Lee Boltin). 142—Drawing by Gamal El-Zoghby. 147—Lion from Procession Way in Babylon, glazed brick, middle First Millennium B.C., The Metropolitan Museum of Art, Fletcher Fund, 1931, New York (Lee Boltin). 148-155—Paintings by Gamal El-Zoghby.

CHAPTER 8: 156—"The Tower of Babel" from *The Book of Hours of the Duke of Bedford*, by an unknown artist, manuscript, 1425-1430, Add. Ms. 18850, courtesy of the Trustees of the British Museum, London (Heinz Zinram). 159—Drawing by Donald and Ann Crews. 161—Elamite head, copper, late Second Millennium B.C., The Metropolitan Museum of Art, Rogers Fund, 1947, New York. 163—"The Lady of Warka," late Fourth Millennium B.C., marble, Iraq Museum, Baghdad (Frank Scherschel). 164-165—Writing tablet, clay, early Second Millennium B.C., courtesy of the Trustees of the British Museum, London; page from the *Haggadah*, Western European, ca. 1900 A.D., The Jewish Museum, New York (Arnold Newman); detail from a copy of the Tomb of Ra'mose, wall painting, early Second Millennium B.C., The Metropolitan Museum of Art, New York—title and opening pages of *L'Apocalypse*, courtesy Joseph Foret, 1961 (Sabine Weiss from Rapho Guillumette); page from the *Urbino Bible*, Vol. II, Attavante degli Attavanti, illuminated manuscript, 1476, Vatican Library (William J. Sumits). 166-167—Four-wheeled chariot, terra cotta model, late Fourth Millennium B.C., Damascus Museum, Syria (David Lees); Attic vase, painted terra cotta, ca. 550 B.C., The Metropolitan Museum of Art, Walter C. Baker Fund, 1916, New York; Egyptian ceramic tile with chariot, blue faïence decorated with black, middle Second Millennium B.C., The Metropolitan Museum of Art, Gift of J. Pierpont Morgan, 1917, New York; "Model T" Ford, Henry Ford Museum, Dearborn, Michigan (Bradley Smith)—Victorian baby carriage, rattan (Bradley Smith)—knight and lord in four-wheeled cart, from France, 13th Century, the Bodleian Library, Oxford (Chanticleer Press)—"Large Bloomer," F. Moore, oil on canvas, 1861, courtesy of the Science Museum, London (Roger Wood). 168—Headdress of Queen Shudu-ad, gold, lapis lazuli and red stone, early Third Millennium B.C., University Museum, Philadelphia (Lee Boltin); mask of an Achaean king from Mycenae, gold, ca. 1580 B.C., National Museum, Athens (Eliot Elisofon)—bust of a Sasanian king (possibly Shapur II), silver gilt, Fourth Century A.D., The Metropolitan Museum of Art, Fletcher Fund, 1965. 169—King Arthur with Three Cardinals from "The Nine Heroes Tapestries," probably by Nicolas Bataille, ca. 1385, The Metropolitan Museum of Art, The Cloisters Collection, Munsey Fund, 1932, Gift of John D. Rockefeller; "Young Elizabeth," Guillem Stretes, oil on canvas (ca. 1559), courtesy of the Earl of Warwick (Dmitri Kessel)—"Louis XIV, King of France," Hyacinthe Rigaud, oil on canvas, 1701, Musée du Louvre, Paris (Eddy van der Veen). 170—Detail from the Law Code of Hammurabi, diorite stele, early Second Millennium B.C., Musée du Louvre, Paris (Cliché Musées Nationaux); detail from "Allegory of Good Government," Ambrogio Lorenzetti, fresco, 1338-1339, Palazzo Pubblico, Siena (Scala, Florence)—"Moses," Rembrandt van Rijn, oil on canvas, 1659, Staatliches Museum, Berlin (Mondadori, Milan). 171—"Trois Avocats," Honoré Daumier, oil on wood, 1854-1856, The Phillips Collection, Washington, D.C. (Henry Beville). 176-177—Drawings by Enid Kotschnig.

# ACKNOWLEDGMENTS

For help given in the preparation of this book, the editors are particularly indebted to Thorkild Jacobsen, Professor of Assyriology, Harvard University. The editors are also indebted to Vaughn E. Crawford, Curator, Department of Ancient Near Eastern Art, The Metropolitan Museum of Art, New York; Robert McC. Adams, Director, Richard Haines, Assistant Professor and Field Architect and Ethel M. Schenk, The Oriental Institute, University of Chicago; George G. Cameron, Professor of Near Eastern Cultures, Chairman of the Department of Near Eastern Languages and Literatures, University of Michigan; William A. Baker, Curator, The Hart Nautical Museum, The Massachusetts Institute of Technology; Harry Bober, Avalon Foundation Professor in the Humanities, Institute of Fine Arts, New York University; Robert H. Dyson, Jr., Associate Curator, and Abdul-Hadi A. Al-Fouadi, University Museum, University of Pennsylvania, Philadelphia; Department of Western Asiatic Antiquities, British Museum, London; André Parrot, Conservateur en Chef du Département des Antiquités Orientales, Musée du Louvre, Paris; Germaine Tureau, Chef de la Section Commerciale du Service Photographique des Musées Nationaux; Hirmer Verlag, Munich; Carlo Pietrangeli, Superintendent Musei Capitolini, Rome; Maristella Bodino, Mondadori Publishing Company, Milan; Madhat Hajj Sirri, Mayor of Baghdad, Iraq; Adnan el Attiya, Chief, Press Section, Ministry of Information, Baghdad, Iraq.

# BIBLIOGRAPHY

*The following volumes and articles were selected during the preparation of this book for their interest and authority, and for their usefulness to readers seeking additional information on specific points. An asterisk (\*) marks works available in both hard cover and paperback editions; a dagger (†) indicates availability only in paperback.*

## GENERAL HISTORY

Adams, Robert M., "The Origin of Cities." *Scientific American*, September 1960.

Beek, Martin A., *Atlas of Mesopotamia*. Thomas Nelson and Sons, 1962.

Braidwood, Robert J., "The Agricultural Revolution." *Scientific American*, September 1960.

*The Cambridge Ancient History*, Fascicles Nos. 1-59.† Rev. ed., Vols. I and II. Cambridge University Press.

Flannery, Kent V., "The Ecology of Early Food Production in Mesopotamia." *Science*, March 12, 1965.

Frankfort, Henri, *The Birth of Civilization in the Near East*.\* Doubleday Anchor Books, 1959.

Hole, Frank, "Investigating the Origins of Mesopotamian Civilization." *Science*, August 5, 1966.

Jacobsen, Thorkild, *The Sumerian King List*.† University of Chicago Press, 1939.

Jastrow, Morris Jr., *The Civilization of Babylonia and Assyria*. J. B. Lippincott, 1915.

Kraeling, Carl H., and Robert M. Adams, eds., *City Invincible: Urbanization and Cultural Development in the Near East*. University of Chicago Press, 1960.

Kramer, Samuel Noah:
"The Sumerians." *Scientific American*, October 1957.
*The Summerians*. University of Chicago Press, 1963.

Luckenbill, D. D., *Ancient Records of Assyria and Babylonia*. 2 vols. University of Chicago Press, 1926.

Macqueen, James G., *Babylon*. Frederick A. Praeger, 1965.

Mallowan, M. E. L., *Early Mesopotamia and Iran*. McGraw-Hill, 1965.

Mellaart, James, *Earliest Civilizations of the Near East*. McGraw-Hill, 1966.

Olmstead, A. T., *History of Assyria*. University of Chicago Press, 1951.

Oppenheim, A. Leo, *Ancient Mesopotamia*. University of Chicago Press, 1964.

Rawlinson, George, *A Memoir of Sir Henry C. Rawlinson*. London, Longmans, Green & Co., 1898.

Roux, Georges, *Ancient Iraq*. World Publishing Company, 1965.

Saggs, H.W.F.:
*Everyday Life in Babylonia and Assyria*. G. P. Putnam's Sons, 1965.
*The Greatness That Was Babylon*. Hawthorn Books, 1966.

Speiser, E. A., ed., *At the Dawn of Civilization*. Rutgers University Press, 1964.

Thesiger, Wilfred, *The Marsh Arabs*. E. P. Dutton, 1964.

## ART AND ARCHITECTURE

Badawy, Alexander, *Architecture in Ancient Egypt and the Near East*. Massachusetts Institute of Technology, 1966.

Frankfort, Henri:
*The Art and Architecture of the Ancient Orient*. 3rd ed. Penguin Books, 1963.
*Cylinder Seals*. Gregg Press, 1965.

Giedion, S., *The Eternal Present: The Beginnings of Architecture*. Pantheon Books, 1964.

Lloyd, Seton, *The Art of the Ancient Near East*.\* Frederick A. Praeger, 1961.

Parrot, André, *The Arts of Mankind*, Vol. 1, *Sumer: The Dawn of Art*, Vol. II, *The Arts of Assyria*. Transl. by Stuart Gilbert and James Emmons. Golden Press, 1961.

Strommenger, Eva, *5000 Years of the Art of Mesopotamia*. Transl. by Christina Haglund, Harry N. Abrams, 1964.

Woolley, Leonard, *The Art of the Middle East*. Crown Publishers, 1961.

## RELIGION, PHILOSOPHY AND LITERATURE

Albright, William Foxwell, *From the Stone Age to Christianity*.\* Doubleday Anchor Books, 1957.

Frankfort, Henri, et al., *The Intellectual Adventure of Ancient Man*. University of Chicago Press, 1946.

Heidel, Alexander, *The Gilgamesh Epic and Old Testament Parallels*.\* University of Chicago Press, 1949.

Kramer, Samuel Noah:
*History Begins at Sumer*. Doubleday Anchor Books, 1959.
*Mythologies of the Ancient World*.\* Doubleday Anchor, 1961.
*Sumerian Mythology*.† Harper Torchbooks, 1961.

Miller, Madeleine S., and J. Lane, *Harper's Bible Dictionary*. 6th ed., Harper & Row, 1959.

Pritchard, James B., ed., *Ancient Near Eastern Texts Relating to the Old Testament*. Princeton University Press, 1955.

## ARCHEOLOGY

Braidwood, Robert J., *Archeologists and What They Do*. Franklin Watts, 1960.

Cameron, George C., "Darius Carved History on Ageless Rock." *National Geographic*, December 1950.

Ehrich, Robert W., ed., *Chronologies in Old World Archaeology*.\* University of Chicago Press, 1965.

Gray, John, *Archaeology and the Old Testament World*.† Harper Torchbooks, 1965.

Kenyon, Kathleen M., *Archaeology in the Holy Land*.\* Frederick A. Praeger, 1960.

King, L. W., and R. C. Thompson, *The Sculptures and Inscription of Darius the Great at Behistûn*. London, British Museum, 1907.

Koldewey, Robert, *The Excavations at Babylon*. Transl. by Agnes S. Johns. London, Macmillan & Co., 1914.

Layard, A. H., *Nineveh and its Remains*. 2 vols. G. P. Putnam, 1849.

Woolley, Leonard:
*Digging up the Past*.† Penguin Books, 1963.
*Excavations at Ur*.\* Barnes & Noble, 1963.
*Ur Excavations*. Vols. II and V. Oxford University Press, 1939.

## WRITING AND TECHNOLOGY

Diringer, David, *Writing*. Frederick A. Praeger, 1962.

Forbes, R. J., *Studies in Ancient Technology*. 9 vols. Leiden, E. J. Brill, 1955-1965.

Gelb, I. J., *A Study of Writing*.\* Rev. ed. University of Chicago Press, 1952.

Singer, Charles, et al., eds., *A History of Technology*, Vol. I, *From Early Times to Fall of Ancient Empires*. Oxford University Press, 1965.

# INDEX

*This symbol in front of a page number indicates an illustration of the subject mentioned.*

## A

A-anne-pad-da, king, 141
Abraham, 35, 158, 161
Abzu (temple), 103; (waters), 107
Adab, city-state, king of, 36; *map* 38
Adadnirari I, king, 57
Agade, 38, 39, 79; *map* 38
Agriculture, 13, 14, 15, 16; development of, 14-16; Sumerian, 42, 45, 47. *See also* Crops; Farmers
Akhenaton, pharaoh, 55
*Akitu* festival, 107-108
Akkad, 38, 60; *map* 9; in Third Millennium B.C., *map* 38
Akkadians: conquest of Sumer, 38-39, 122; culture, *chart* 54; schools, 122-123. *See also* languages: Akkadian
Alabaster, 11, 60, 142, 143, 144
Albright, W. F., 161
Alexander the Great, 120, 154, 168
Amanus Mountains, 38, 62; *map* 8
Amorites, 51, 55; conquest of Sumer, 38, 40, 51-52; *map* 38
An, god, 100, 101, 104, 111, 140
Anatolia, 14, 54, 55, 124, 159; *map* 8
An-ki (universe), 99
Animals: in art, *42-43, *63-69, *98, *138, 140, 144; domesticated, 13, 14, 16, 31, *42-43, *45, 88, 131; products, 145-146
Anunnaki, gods, 105,111
Aqarquf (ancient Dur-Kurigalzu), 55
Arabian Desert, *maps* 9, 38
Arabians, 72, 73
Arabs, marsh. *See* Marsh Arabs
Aramaeans, 56, 57, 59
Archeologists: activities at Nippur, *20-23; at Ur, 176; dating of artifacts, 23, 26, 28, 176-177; determination of date of site, *23; reconstruction of culture and life, 12, 13, 15, 17-18, 85, 86; treatment of artifacts, *25-27; use of flying camera, *28-29. *See also* specific locations, countries and places
Architecture, 11, 139-143, 157; Babylon, *147-155; city, 79-80. *See also* Houses; Palaces; Temples; Ziggurats
Armenia, 55, 56, 59, 60, 62, 85; *map* 9
Armies, 80, 86; Assyrian, 57-58, 60, 71, 72-73, 75; infantry, *48-49, 71; Sumerian, 38, 39, 49. *See also* Battles; Soldiers
Arms, 45, 57, 58, 144
Arthur, king, 168, *169
Arts, 138-146. *See also* Architecture; Friezes; Inlay; Mosaics; Pottery; Reliefs; Sculpture; Seals; Tiles
Arvad, 56; *map* 59
Ashkelon: *map* 59
Assur, city, 52, 53, 56, 62, 143; *maps* 8, 58, 59, 126
Assur, god, 64, 66, 76, 107
Assurbanipal, Assyrian king, 62-67, 72, 73, *76-77, 143; as hunter, *63-67;

library, 123; as priest, *68-69; as warrior, *72-75
Assurnasirpal II, king, 51, 57-58
Assursharrat, queen, *77
Assuruballit, king, 55
Assyria: Assurbanipal's realm, Seventh Century B.C., *map* 59; conquests of, 61, 62; cruelty in wars, 57, 58, 62; culture, *chart* 54; Kassite claims, 54-55; *map* 9; reign of Assurbanipal, 62-67; reign of Assurnasirpal II, 57-58, 60; reign of Esarhaddon, 61-62; reign of Sargon II, reign of Sennacherib, 61-62; reign of Shalmaneser III, 59; reign of Tiglath-Pileser I, 56-57; III, 59-60; reign of Tukulti-Ninurta, 56, 60; relations with Egypt, 55, 60, 61; revolts, 57, 61, 62, 95; rise to power, 55-56, 57
Astrology, 126, 159
Astronomy, 125, 159

## B

Babylon, 53, 79; capture, 54, 56, 62, 151, 154; destructions of, 61-62, 72; Esagila (temple), 108; excavations, 12, *141, *147-155; hanging gardens, 62; Ishtar gateway, 108, *150-151; *maps* 9, 58, 59; New Year Festival, 107-108; Tower of Babel, 62, *148-149, *154-155
Babylonia: *map* 9; conquests, 54-55, 56, 60, 61; culture, *chart* 54; Hammurabi's realm, 18th Century B.C., *map* 58; Nebuchadrezzar II's realm, 62, *map* 59; reign of Hammurabi, 52-53; reign of Nabonidus, 62; reign of Nebuchadrezzar, 52, 147-155; revolts against Assyria, 61-62
Baghdad, 12, 16, 31, 35, 52, 55, 140, 147; *map* 9
Battles, 80; in art, *41, 142, 144; Assyria, *72-75; Sumerian, *41, *48-49
Behistun, Rock of, 119, 120-121, *136-137
Bitumen, 92, *93, 142, 145
Borsippa, 108; *map* 38
Braidwood, Robert J., excavations, 13-14
Bricks, 22, *32, 79, 85, 140, 141, 142; brickmakers, 145, 146; enameled and glazed, 62, 142, *147, 151, *152-153; mud, 13, *17, *32, 33, 34, *74-75, 79, 85, 142
Bridges, *149
Bulls, 60, 108, *115, 128, *138, 139, 143, 150, 159
Burnaburiash, king, 55
Byblos, 56; *maps* 8, 59

## C

Calah (modern Nimrud), 58-59, 60, 79, 143; *maps* 9, 59

Calendar, 35, 125
Canaanites, 123, 158, 159
Canals, 33, 34, *37, 47, 61. *See also* Irrigation
Carbon 14 dating, 15, 28, 177
Carchemish, *maps* 8, 59
Caspian Sea, *maps* 9, 58, 59
Cattle, 13, 14, 16, *42-43, 51, 111, 122, *138, 139
Caucasus Mountains, 62, 146
Chaldea and Chaldeans, 57, 60, 61; conquest of Assyria, 62; culture, *chart* 54
Chariots, 55; Assyrian, 57, 60, *64; Egyptian, 166, *167; Sumerian, 38, *48-49
Cilicia, 59; *map* 59
Cities and towns, 11, 13, 14-15, 16, 17, 80-86; dating, *23, 176-177; government, 34-35, 86; Palestine, 14-15; Sumer, 33-34. *See also* Urban development
City-states, 31, 35, 36, 47, 51, 52, 159
Clay tablets. *See* Tablets, clay
Climate, 11, 31, 85
Copper, 16, 49, 58, 85, 141, 143, 146, 161
Costumes, *78
Crafts and craftsmen, 45, 83, 101, *138-146
Creation of heaven and earth, 100-101, 103, 160; *Enuma-Elish* epic, 107-108; myth, *110-111
Crops, 13, 14, 16, 42, 84, 92, 145
Cultures: chronological chart, 54
Cuneiform writing, 12, 40, 55, 85, 86, 131, 158, 164; deciphering, 20, 119-122, 136; development, 122, *132-133, 135; spread, 122-123; Rock of Behistun, 119, 120-121, *136-137; types, *118, 120, 121-123, *134-135. *See also* Tablets, clay
Cylinder seals. *See* Seals, cylinder
Cyprus, 159; *maps* 8, 59
Cyrus, Persian king, 62

## D

Damascus, 59, 60; *map* 59
Darius, Persian king, 120, *136; inscriptions on Rock of Behistun, 121-122, *136-137
Dead Sea, 14; *map* 8
Death and afterlife, 99, 100, 105-107, 135, 160, 162
Dilmun, 103-104
*Dingir* (god), 100
Divination, 126
Diyala River, 141; *maps* 9, 38, 58
Dumuzi, king and god, 35, 106-107
Dur-Kurigalzu (modern Aqarquf), 55
Dur-Sharrukin (modern Khorsabad), 60, 79, 143; excavations, 12, 143; *maps* 9, 59

## E

Eannatum, king, 36-37
Ecbatana, 119; *map* 59
*Edubba* (school), 122-126
Egypt, 38, 103, 123; Assyrian conquest, 61; culture, *chart* 54; hieroglyphics, 119, *165; influence of Mesopotamia, 157-158; *maps* 58, 59; reign of Akhenaton, 55; relations with Assyria, 60, 61
Elam, 158, 161; conquest, *74-75, 77; *maps* 9, 59
Elamites, 51, 158; alliance against Assyria, 72; conquests, 36, 38, 40, 56, 60; culture, *chart* 54; kings, 75, *76, 161; writing, 120-121; *map* 38
Elburz Mountains, *map* 9
Elizabeth I, queen, 168, *169
Enki, god, 100, *101, 105, 111, 113; in myths, 103-104, 106, 107

Enkidu, *114-115, 128
Enlil, god, 53, 100, 105, 111; myths, 101-103, 104, *116
Erech (modern Warka), 35, 37, 101, 128, 176-177; city goddess, 103, 106, 107; excavations, 12, *28-29, 38; kings, 35, 36, 38, 39, 106, 109; *maps* 9, 38; temples, 140-144; walls, 79
Ereshkigal, goddess, 105, 106, 113
Eridu, 33; city god, 102, 103; excavations, 34, 139, 140, 142; *maps* 9, 38
Esarhaddon, king, 61-62
Eshnunna, 52, 53, 55; conquest, 53, 55; excavations, 141, 142; *maps* 9, 38, 58
Etana, king, 35
Euphrates River, 11, 19, 31, 38, 56, 61, 103, 108, 112, 147, 149, 176; *maps* 9, 38, 58, 59
Excavations. *See* Archeologists; specific locations

## F

Farmers, 31, *42-43, 83, 85; almanac, 84, 162; implements, 14, 145, 159
Farming. *See* Agriculture
Festivals and feasts, 34, 106-108, 144
Fish, 31, *45, 103; marsh Arabs, 87, *94-95
Floods, 33, 92, 128, 149, 161, 176; myths, 104, *116
Food, 13, 15, 33, 80, 83, 135, 139. *See also* Grains and cereals
Friezes, 140, 142, *152-153

## G

Gaza, 60; *map* 59
Geshtinanna, goddess, 107
Gilgamesh, king and god, 36, 39, 105, *109, 112, *138, 139; Epic of, 36, 79, *114-115, 128
Girsu, *map* 38
Glassmaking and glazing, 62, 142, 146, *147, 151, *152-153
Goats, 13, 16, 31, *42, *98, 145
Gods and goddesses, *10, 11, 83, 126-127; Assyrian, *50, 51, 64, 66, 68, 70, 77, 107; Babylonian, 32, 53, 56, 62, 88, 107-108, 151, 154; as city protectors, 34, 80, 101, 102, 103; divination, 126; Egyptian, 55; epic tales, 107-108; eye-idol, *105; household, 34, 84, 145; myths, 101-104, 106-107, *110-111, *112-113, *116; pantheon, 35, 53, 100, 104; personal, 105, 161; relation to man, 104-105, 139, 140; rites and festivals honoring, 34, 86, *98, 106-108, 139, 144; Sumerian (*dingir*), *10, 11, 35, 39, 53, 87. *See also* Myths; specific deities; Religion; Temples
Gold, 11, 12, 39, 58, 61, 79, 85, 98, 142, 143, 146
Government: cities and towns, 34-35; state, 47, 80, 86, 136, 160
Grains and cereals, 13, 16, 42, *44, 45, 83-84, 85, 122, 131, 144
Greece: influence of Mesopotamia, 159, 160, 161
Grotefend, Georg F., 120, 121
Gudea, prince, 39, *118, 141, 143
Gutians: conquest of Sumer, 38, 39; *map* 38

## H

Halaf, culture, 16
Halys River: *maps* 58, 59

✕

PRODUCTION STAFF FOR TIME INCORPORATED

*John L. Hallenbeck (Vice President and Director of Production),*
*Robert E. Foy, Caroline Ferri and Don Sheldon*
*Text photocomposed under the direction of Albert J. Dunn and Arthur J. Dunn.*